TV Dinners

40 Classic TV Kid Stars Dish Up Favorite Recipes with a Side of Memories

By Laurie Jacobson

For information, please address TV Classics Press, a Division of Micro Publishing Media,
Inc, PO Box 1522, Stockbridge, MA 01262. TV Classics Press books may be purchased for
sales promotional purposes. For information email info@micropublishingmedia.com.
Designed by Deborah Herman and Jane McWhorter

ISBN 978-1-944068-91-2

TV Classics Press is a Division of Micro Publishing Media, Inc.
We specialize in nostalgia and pictorial fan books.
You can follow us on facebook and Instragram.
Please review our catalog at micropublishingmedia.com

This book is lovingly dedicated to child actors everywhere. Your road is not an easy one. Your sacrifices are great, but oh, the lovely light you leave behind.

Foreword
By Paul Petersen

When you come into people's living rooms once a week, people understandably feel they know you. And so it was in the mid-'50s when television took over the world of entertainment. Three networks, 100 million television sets. For kids who were featured on the many shows that drew entire families into the living room, the effects were immediate... and unprecedented. Fame, real Fame on a level only rarely seen in the world of motion pictures, became a suffocating reality.

Kid actors suddenly found themselves the center of attention when they went to the movies, shopping, even just walking down the street. Airports became a gauntlet of autographs and hurriedly snapped pictures. You had to attend family gatherings, so your cousins and shirt-tail relations didn't think you were "stuck up." And fan mail came in over-sized canvas bags.

For the guys, meeting girls got easier. For girls, the dating world became perilous, indeed since every hormonal male wanted to be "the first." I got a black eye now and then standing up for my big TV sister, Shelley Fabares.

My father, an engineer at Lockheed, accurately summed up the process. "I used to love it when I could introduce you as my son...but I hated it when I was introduced as your father."

And everywhere the same words: "Don't let this go to your head."
Yeah, right.

Say what you will about the famous kids working the sunny side of the street in Hollywood in the Golden Era of television. They knew where to hang out.

In the Hollywood of the '50s, young actors didn't have a lot of opportunities to socialize. Often we'd see each other on auditions and despite the competitive situation, find the time to visit. You might meet up at the Work Permit office downtown; or, if you already had a regular job on a series, at one of the rare events that brought the well-known kids together like the Hollywood Christmas Lane parade or an arranged gathering where our various publicity agents got us together for roller skating, bowling or a traditional pool party. What a pack we were–fifteen or twenty kid stars from mostly television shows like *Lassie*, *Father Knows Best*, *Leave it to Beaver*, *The Mickey Mouse Club*, *Dennis the Menace*…a pack of puppies learning as we went.

This was long before the days of Craft Service (a company that caters an array of food throughout the day on the set.) Food is now provided by the Producers. When you worked (in the '50s), you went out for lunch; once it was time to eat, you had choices to make. If you were in the Valley, it was DuPar's or the Hot Dog Show. If you were in Hollywood at CBS Television Center, you headed for Farmer's Market or Canter's Deli. The circuit of favored restaurants ran past all the major studios, commercial houses, and dance studios. For us, these places were about more than the great food; it was a chance to get out of the dark, stale soundstage, to feel the bright, warm California sun on your skin…and to see some girls.

What fun, those Good Ol' Days as a working kid actor in Old Hollywood…

Paul Petersen
Jeff Stone on *The Donna Reed Show*

Introduction

Growing up in the '50s and '60s was a pretty swell time for most Baby Boomers. Television was still a new and wondrous delight broadcasting shows in black and white with orange tubes glowing in the back and funny "rabbit ears" on top that had to be adjusted just right. During the Golden Age of Television, just three channels ruled the airwaves. That meant, in 1960, when 90% of American homes had TVs, about 55 million people watched each show every week for years! With all the channels that exist today, that is a phenomenon unique to one generation and will never be repeated.

And long before streaming, or DVRs or even VCRs, family members came running from all corners at the appointed time to gather in front of often the only TV set in the home to enjoy their favorite programs together. For many, watching them became a family tradition.

Today, a plethora of nostalgic networks allow Boomers to enjoy their favorite shows again with their children and grandchildren. Families continue to bond watching Classic TV series and the kids who starred in them. These icons and the characters they played are firmly embedded in our popular culture, cherished by millions of loyal fans who continue to celebrate them. We didn't just watch those kids grow up, we grew up with them. They are an indelible part of the fabric of our lives.

To this very day, the shared experience of watching these kid stars continues to connect us with family, with friends, and even with complete strangers. If someone shouts "Danger, Will Robinson!" we freeze in our tracks. When a Boomer says, "He's a real Eddie Haskell," we know EXACTLY what that means! We were all part of the "peanut gallery." We all sent in soup labels and cereal box tops for secret decoder rings and other treasures. Everyone knew how to spell Mickey Mouse. The kids on television were thought of as best friends and blood brothers. Their photos hung in bedrooms and school lockers across the nation.

At a time before society was so connected, these kids *were* the connection for millions of people. The Mouseketeers got it right when they sang their closing theme: "Now it's time to say goodbye to all our family…" We were family. That's how we felt.

And as our extended family, having dinner with our TV best friends just seemed natural. Swanson even developed a packaged meal to eat while watching them called a TV dinner. It fit nicely on a folding table called a TV tray which was the perfect height for dining while sitting on the couch. That's what many of us did, but what did the kids we were watching do? What did they eat back then…and where? For that matter, what do they eat today? I asked 40 of them to share their favorite dishes from then and now—some passed down through their families, others from restaurants now extinct, but all served with a side of delicious memories that provides glimpses into their lives both as child stars and as adults. Hope you brought your appetite!

Laurie Jacobson
Santa Rosa, CA

Laurie Jacobson is a celebrated Hollywood historian, writer, and reformed stand-up comic. She has authored *Hollywood Heartbreak*, *Hollywood Haunted*, *Dishing Hollywood* and *Timmy's in the Well—The Jon Provost Story* as well as having contributed to several other tomes on Hollywood history.

She has written and produced documentaries, television series and specials, including *The 20th Anniversary of the Mary Tyler Moore Show*, *The Museum of Television and Radio's Salute to Funny Women of Television*, *The Warner Bros. Studio Rededication Party*, *The Suzanne Somers Show*, *Photoplay* and *Hollywood Chronicles*. For nearly a decade, she served as head of development for legendary producer Jack Haley, Jr.

As a reigning expert on Tinseltown mysteries, scandals, and ghosts, Laurie appears regularly on television, podcasts and radio. In 2017, the Southern California Motion Picture Council presented her with their Lifetime Achievement Award for her outstanding literary contributions in the entertainment industry. She and husband Jon Provost make their home in Northern California.

1950s

No singular invention changed American life more in the 1950s than television. Regional and societal divisions faded as the country discovered they shared values, dreams…and a lot of laughter. *I Love Lucy* ruled. Popular sitcoms like *Leave It to Beaver*, *The Donna Reed Show* and *Father Knows Best* presented perfect families with briefcase-toting dads bidding goodbye to perfectly coiffed moms while the kids created mischief, but always learned their lesson.

And speaking of kids, an array of shows was made just for them like *The Mickey Mouse Club* and its serial, *Spin and Marty*. Westerns were huge; and nothing could beat the adventures of a boy and his dog. Yes, the '50s was a great time to grow up with TV.

Dennis the Menace

Dennis the Menace follows the antics of the well-meaning but mischievous Dennis Mitchell. The series starred Jay North as Dennis Mitchell; Herbert Anderson as his father, Henry; Gloria Henry as his mother, Alice; Joseph Kearns as George Wilson and Sylvia Field as his wife, Martha; Gale Gordon took over as George's brother, John Wilson after Kearns's death with Sara Seegar as his wife, Eloise; and Jeannie Russell as Dennis's friend, Margaret. It ran four seasons on CBS on Sunday evenings from October 4, 1959, to July 7, 1963, for a total of 146 episodes.

Jay North

Jay North was 7 years old when he was chosen to be the TV personification of the Hank Ketcham comic strip, *Dennis the Menace*. He'd already been working steadily for years by then as a child model and actor in commercials and small parts on a number of variety shows like *The George Gobel Show, The Eddie Fisher Show,* and *The Milton Berle Show.* The success of those appearances led to bigger roles on popular series like *Wanted: Dead or Alive* starring Steve McQueen, *77 Sunset Strip, Rescue 8, Cheyenne, Bronco, Colt .45,* and *Sugarfoot.* And he'd made appearances on the big screen in *The Miracle of the Hills* and *The Big Operator.*

Then, in June 1958, Jay auditioned for *Dennis.* Hank Ketcham chose Jay personally over 500 others. Jay filmed a pilot that summer with Herbert Anderson, Gloria Henry, and Joseph Kearns. But close to a year passed before they moved forward with the series. *Dennis the Menace* premiered on Sunday, October 4, 1959, and was an instant smash.

Jay's father left when he was four. While his mother worked, his aunt and uncle had charge of him both on the set and off. Jay's personal life, however, was far from happy. His aunt and uncle were cruel to him both emotionally and physically. As his workload increased, he was forced to travel regularly with them on weekends to promote the show.

In addition to the series, North appeared as Dennis in commercials for the show's sponsors, Kellogg's cereals, as well as Best Foods mayonnaise, Skippy peanut butter and Bosco chocolate milk. He also guested on television shows like *The Donna Reed Show* and *The Red Skelton Hour* and in the feature film *Pépé.*

Near the end of season three, Joseph Kearns, Dennis's exasperated neighbor, Mr. Wilson, suddenly died. For season four, the wonderful Gale Gordon came on board as Mr. Wilson's brother, but it was a blow to the show. And Jay, now 11, had begun to outgrow the role. Ratings dipped; and in the spring of 1963, *Dennis the Menace* was canceled.

Jay attended school but continued to pursue work throughout the '60s, guesting on *Wagon Train*, *The Man from U.N.C.L.E*, *My Three Sons* and *The Lucy Show* with his former co-star, Gale Gordon. It was a constant battle to avoid being typecast in roles similar to *Dennis*. He landed the lead in family films *Zebra in the Kitchen* (1965) and *Maya* (1966) the latter shot in India. In 1967, he returned to India for a year to star in a TV series based on the film.

When Jay returned to L.A., he and his *Maya* co-star, Sajid Kahn, were popular teen idols featured in posters and magazines. But Jay had missed a year of school, and now back in Hollywood, he had difficulty keeping up. Film and TV work was scarce, but he found work as a voice actor for animated television series, *The Banana Splits Adventure Hour* and a teenaged Bamm-Bamm Rubble on *The Pebbles and Bamm-Bamm Show*.

Struggling emotionally to deal with both the abuse he suffered at the hands of his aunt and uncle as well as an industry that had failed to protect him, Jay left Hollywood in 1971. Several years later, he enlisted in the US Navy. He left with an honorable discharge in 1979 and, once again, returned to Los Angeles, a bitter, unhappy man.

Paul Petersen, the founder of A Minor Consideration, reached out to help him secure his footing. A grateful Jay was able to find

Sajid and Jay

himself in giving back to others, providing advice and counseling to a new generation of child actors. He also began attending fan conventions with his dear friend and co-star, Jeanne Russell, where he reunited with many old friends.

Since the early 1990s, North has made occasional appearances on talk shows, in documentaries and in cameos on *The Simpsons* and in the David Spade comedy feature *Dickie Roberts: Former Child Star.*

Jon Provost, Lassie and Jay

I liked to add a little yellow mustard. The chili had a kick, and the mustard cooled it down.

He and his wife moved to Florida, where Jay worked for years as a prison guard. He is now happily retired.

"My favorite thing as a kid was sneaking off campus from Marion Colbert's School with my best friend, Jon Provost. The school was on Fairfax Avenue between Melrose and Beverly. We'd walk up to Beverly to Pink's, a hot dog stand, family-owned…it's still there after 75 years. We'd get chili cheese dogs and walk to a nearby park to chow down on them…a fat dog in a bun smothered in chili with grated cheddar cheese melted over the top.

As an adult, I eat a little differently. I have to admit I never really had much interest in cooking or the kitchen. Fortunately, my wife enjoys it, and she created this great dish I ask for often."

Jay's Favorite Broccoli Casserole

1 pkg frozen 1 lb fresh broccoli chopped or spears—Cook, cool and drain
2 eggs beaten
1 cup mayo
1 can cream of celery soup
½ cup milk
1 cup sharp cheese, grated
1 tbsp Worcestershire sauce
Salt and pepper
1 tbsp. Onion flakes

Mix all ingredients and stir in broccoli
Butter the bottom of a casserole dish and pour in mixture. Top with Ritz crackers and dot with butter.
Bake 40-45 minutes at 350 degrees

Jeanne Russell

Jeanne Russell moved to Hollywood when she was just 2 years old from Washington state and grew up literally in the shadow of the studios. She describes the lifestyle with her parents and brother, Bryan, as vaudevillian. Her father was a tenor, her mother an accompanist and heir living room was filled with performers and show biz types.

"We lived on a street called Fernwood right in back of the studio. In those days, there were no big parking lots, so the studio personnel parked on the street. One day there was a knock on the door. A production secretary from the *Lassie* set said they needed a small boy to do some pick- up shots. They had spotted Bryan on the street. Would he be interested in doing it? They knocked on the right door. My parents and grandmother took Bryan over to the set. All he had to do was hold up a can of Campbell's soup. They needed a little hand and didn't want to pull Jon (Provost) out of school.

As the magical, mysterious physical break in Hollywood went down, Cecile (Jon's mother) started talking to my grandmother on the set, and those two clicked; they were like kindred souls. My grandmother was very much into health foods. In the '50s, she was culturing her own yogurt and pressing her own carrot juice. And as a French war bride who moved to Alabama, she also cooked Southern so those two clicked instantly.

My grandmother said, "When Jon has a break, why don't you come over to our place? Jon can get out of the set atmosphere. I'll feed him some good food; he can play with the kids." When that started happening, Cecile said that whenever they needed extras, she would make sure we were used. That was how our break took off. It takes someone like that to put you under their wing. She sort of shepherded us into the business…and being in show business has defined my whole life. So Cecile's like my show business fairy godmother!"

About that time, they met an agent, and both Jeanne and Bryan worked quite a bit—Bryan in film and Jeannie on TV. She appeared in popular shows like *Death Valley Days* and *The Deputy*. She also appeared on Dinah Shore's show; but she is best remembered as Margaret Wade, playmate of Dennis Mitchell on *Dennis the Menace*.

One of her first auditions after the series ended was with legendary director Alfred Hitchcock. She was cast in his highly acclaimed film *The Birds*, but when she arrived at the Northern California location, she discovered she was more or less an extra, one of the school children running from the vicious feathered creatures. Once an actor had been a series regular, he or she never accepted extra work; but Jeannie was there, so she just went with it. And she's very glad she did. It was an amazing experience for her with a mechanical bird strapped to her back. She pulled a string as she ran in terror, which made the bird peck her head, actually drawing blood. Recently, Jeanne was invited back to Bodega Bay to speak of her experiences working with the master of suspense.

Jeanne's last gig as a child actor came when she was 16. Working with children was a big expense for a show. Not only did they pay the child's salary, but they paid for a teacher on set and a social worker as well. And kids had restrictions on the hours they could work. Once kids hit their teens, unless you were a big name like, say Natalie Wood, it was more lucrative and a lot easier for a show to hire an 18-year-old who could play 16. That was the problem child actors like Jeannie faced. But unlike many of her peers, Jeannie's parents saved all her earnings. That made all the difference for her. She went to college and re-directed her energy.

Since 1978, Jeanne has had her own chiropractic practice in the San Fernando Valley of Los Angeles. But that was not the end of her involvement in the business. She has done live theater, and soundtrack work as well as performing as a singer. In the 1990s, Russell was active on the national talk show and news feature circuit. In 1993, she made a cameo appearance in the film version of *Dennis the Menace* playing one of the Mitchells' neighbors. Jeanne and Jay are still dear friends and occasionally appear together at celebrity events when schedules allow.

Jay North and Jeannie Russell Today

More importantly, Jeannie devoted a good deal of her time to children working in the business. She joined forces with fellow child actor Paul Petersen, founder of A Minor Consideration, fighting for child labor laws and fairer practices for working minors. She has spoken to many groups sharing her knowledge and expertise based on her personal experience. And she co-chaired the Screen Actors Guild (SAG) Young Performers' Committee for several years. She is very grateful for her working years and for the opportunity to give back.

"I was one of the chosen," she proudly declares. "I'm a card-carrying member of the tribe forever. My work remains. I was part of classic television."

Jeanne with some of her tribe: (From left) Bill Mumy, Barry Livingston, Paul Petersen, Stan Livingston, Tony Dow, Billy Gray, Jon Provost

My Mother's Southern Fried Chicken

"She would wash off the cut-up chicken, salt and pepper it and put it in a brown paper bag full of flour. She would then fry it in hot oil in a cast-iron skillet. When it was the perfect golden brown, she drained it on another brown paper bag.

I always teased her that her secret ingredient was the beer she consumed while frying it up.

As an adult, my favorite dish to take to holiday dinners is:

Aunt Jewell's Carrot and Cheese Casserole

This is also a Southern dish. Aunt Jewell was my Cousin Laura's mother's sister—one of the five Darby sisters. She made this on one of my visits to Alabama, 'visitin' at the Lake' and it was love at first bite. Laura eventually gave me the recipe, and every time I bring it somewhere, I am always asked to bring it again.

Aunt Jewell's Carrot and Cheese Casserole serves 6

1 lb carrots

diced and cooked in boiling water until tender then drain and set aside.
In mixing bowl mix:

1/2 cup chopped onion
2/3 cup mayonnaise
1 teaspoon sugar
1 cup grated sharp cheddar cheese

Add drained carrots and mix well. Put in a buttered casserole.
Top with buttered bread crumbs.
Bake at 350 until bubbling hot (approximately 30 minutes)"

The Donna Reed Show

The Donna Reed Show starred Donna Reed as middle-class housewife Donna Stone and dealt with typical family issues of the day. Carl Betz co-starred as her pediatrician husband, Dr. Alex Stone with Shelley Fabares and Paul Petersen as their teenage children, Mary and Jeff. Petersen's younger sister, Patty Petersen, joined the cast as adopted daughter Trisha in 1963. The show ran eight seasons from September 24, 1958 through March 19, 1966 with 275 episodes.

Paul Petersen

In child actor circles, Paul Petersen is known as the Big Kahuna, the Daddy of them all and Fearless Leader—not just because of his outstanding career, but for the incredible work he has done on their behalf after the cameras stopped rolling.

Former child star, pop singer, writer, spokesman and child rights activist, father and grandfather, Paul was born in 1945 in Glendale, California, and was pushed into the business by a determined stage mother. "I became a child actor because my mom was bigger than I was." He began performing at 8 as an original Mouseketeer on *The Mickey Mouse Club* in 1955. He also appeared in movies like *Houseboat* with Cary Grant and Sophia Loren.

In 1958, at age 12, he won the role of Donna Reed's son, Jeff Stone, on her popular sitcom, *The Donna Reed Show*. With Carl Betz as his highly practical doctor dad and Shelley Fabares as his pretty older sister, the foursome became the ideal nuclear family for late '50s/early '60s viewers. The series ran for 8 years and Paul literally grew up on camera making a smooth transition to his teens. Fan clubs for him sprouted up everywhere, and his photos adorned the bedroom walls of teenaged girls coast to coast. So popular were both Paul and Shelley that they spun off into recording careers, to become singing idols despite their modest voices. She scored with the #1 hit, "Johnny Angel," and he had a few hits with "She Can't Find Her Keys," "Keep Your Love Locked," "Lollipops and Roses," and "My Dad."

He has played important television roles in *Playhouse 90*, *Lux Video Theatre*, *Ford Theatre*, *G.E. Theater*. He was voted "Most Photographed Teenager in Show Business" by the Professional Photographers Assoc., "Best Dressed Teenager in Show Business" by CALMAC, "Best Teen Actor on Television" by *16 Magazine* and "Outstanding Young Star Of The Year" by the Harlequinade Awards

The fun ended, however, after the show's demise in 1966. There were roles in *A Time for Killing* and J*ourney to Shiloh*, guest parts on *The Virginian* and *The F.B.I.* and the role of Moondoggie in a revamped *Gidget* TV movie, *Gidget Grows Up*. But as it was for most child stars, the roles eventually stopped coming.

Lost and abandoned, Paul eventually was forced to give it all up, experiencing a period of great personal anguish and turmoil. Wisely, he enrolled in college. In the mid-'70s, he decided to embark on a writing career. His first publication was a non-fiction book on high performance racecar driving, followed by eight fictional action-adventure books in a series called *The Smuggler*. In 1977, he penned a biographical work about the original Mousketeers, *Walt, Mickey and Me*. He wrote 16 books in all. His most recent is a scrapbook called *The Donna Reed Show: A Pictorial Memoir* in which he shares memories of his time on the iconic show.

Of his many accomplishments, his biggest to date, however, has been to give back, selflessly, to an industry that unceremoniously dumped him. Today, Paul is the most dedicated advocate in protecting both present-day and past child stars. Paul formed A Minor Consideration, a child-actor support group back in 1990, and it has had a tremendously positive and profound effect in Hollywood.

In essence, A Minor Con is an outreach organization that oversees the emotional, financial and legal protection of kids and former kids in show business. Among the issues Paul deals with are better education and stricter laws regarding a 40-hour workweek. For those who have "been there, done that" and are experiencing severe emotional and/or substance abuse problems, he offers a solid hand in helping them find a renewed sense of purpose.

Paul lives in Los Angeles with his wife, Rana, a studio lot nurse for 44 years, 42 of them at CBS Studio Center in Studio City.

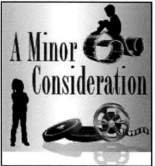

"Remembering the food I craved, it comes down to chili dogs at the Hot Dog Show at Ventura Blvd and Coldwater Canyon—long gone now. Four dogs (!) with chili and onions (no cheese) with an order of fries.

The Hot Dog Show was kitty-corner from Bob's Big Boy in Toluca Lake, and it always came down to parking. If Bob's was busy, I went to the Hot Dog Show. I drove either my Cobra convertible or the little red Volkswagon Beetle Donna Reed gave me.

Age and necessity have forced me to eat healthier these days. Here's a favorite recipe in our house.

Paul and Rana's Healthy Gluten-Free Meatloaf

(serves 4)

1 1/2 lb ground turkey
1/2 lb ground beef
1 egg
1 cup gluten-free potato chips

(use a roller to mash them into flakes in a plastic freezer bag).
Add chopped onions and garlic to taste.
Mix all in a large bowl.
Shape to fit an oiled meatloaf pan.
Use fingers to make a trough in the top of that loaf.
Bake at 350 degrees for 1 3/4 hrs.
Remove and add ketchup into the trough.
Bake for another 15 minutes at 375 degrees.
Remove, let cool for ten minutes before slicing.

I like the crispy ends and you'll have plenty left over for meatloaf sandwiches if you're cooking for two!"

Father Knows Best

Father Knows Best starred Robert Young, Jane Wyatt, Elinor Donahue, Billy Gray, and Lauren Chapin as the Andersons, a very likable middle-class family living in the mythical Midwestern town of Springfield. The series aired for six seasons with a total of 203 episodes from October of 1954 through September 17, 1960, on CBS and NBC.

Billy Gray

Billy Gray is an L.A. boy, born and raised. His mother, Beatrice, was an actress and often brought her young son along to her auditions. Her agent saw a special spark in 5-year-old Billy and began sending him on auditions. The kid nailed almost everything he went out for, appearing in dozens of bit parts like paperboys or one of a group with a line or two. The turning point came at 13 when he was cast in *On Moonlight Bay* with Doris Day. The film's success brought Billy bigger parts, including his favorite, the role of Bobby Benson in *The Day the Earth Stood Still* with the great Patricia Neal as his mother.

He continued to be seen in TV shows like *Annie Oakley*, *The Loretta Young Show*, *Adventures of Superman* and much more until 1954 when he landed the plum role of Bud Anderson in the classic series *Father Knows Best*, already a popular radio show. Producers had tested over 100 teenage boys for the part. Billy, 15, was called back two or three times, then shot a test scene with the entire Anderson family around the supper table. That cinched it.

Billy was Bud Anderson during its six-season run. In 1959, he was nominated for an Emmy for Best Supporting Actor.

During the run of the show and for a few years after, Billy continued to appear in films and on TV: *The Seven Little Foys, Some Like It Hot, Peter Gunn, Bachelor Father, The Alfred Hitchcock Show, The Red Skelton Hour, Rawhide, Combat!, I Spy, Medical Center.* But when the series ended, he ran into some trouble. A baggie with seeds and stems from marijuana was found in his car. He was tried and sentenced to 1-10 years. He served 45 days, followed by a probationary period. At that time, a vicious rumor circulated that Billy was a heroin addict. Anyone who knew him knew otherwise, but offers of acting work virtually evaporated. For Billy, it was a golden opportunity that led to something he called "the best thing that ever happened to me." He discovered speedway—a motorcycle sport on a flat, oval track of loosely packed dirt and shale. Four to six riders compete. The bikes have no brakes as they slip and "powerslide" around the curves on the edge of disaster. Billy loved it, couldn't get enough. And he was great at it. In fact, he won the 1977 National Long Track Speedway Ascot One Half Mile Dirt Oval Championship.

As a competitive Class A Speedway motorcycle racer, he rode 3 nights a week for 23 years. He was well-known and well-respected on the race circuit and rode well into his late forties. "It's driven me crazy for decades that such an elegant and noble activity has not received the attention and monetary reward that it deserves," wrote Billy in a TV proposal for the sport.

Incredibly creative, Billy is always thinking. His mind is never idle. He has invented a wide variety of products; and is co-owner of Big Rock Engineering, creators of innovative guitar accessories, and other products. He has loved every moment of his ride in life, wouldn't change anything about it. And at 82, he is still power sliding around the next curve.

"I was living in Pacific Palisades when 'FKB' started its TV run, and there was an ice cream parlor called Dilly's, which was short for the owner's name, Mr. Dilahunt. He made his ice cream sooo rich that after eating a scoop, I swear there was an eighth-of-an inch thick coating of butter on the roof of your mouth you could scrape off with a spoon. I went there a lot. I still dream about that ice cream.

As a kid, I worked on a lot of Westerns and, on locations, the catering trucks could always be relied upon to come up with a fabulous fried egg sandwich.

Billy's Favorite Fried Egg Sandwich

In the trucks, everything is cooked on a griddle. You can use two separate frying pans. In one, put 2 pieces of bread and lots of butter. Toast on both sides over low heat.

In the other pan, melt butter and fry 2 eggs until the yolks are almost about done the way you like them. Place a slice of cheese over each egg. When cheese melts, place each egg side by side on one slice of bread. Salt and pepper to taste. Cover with the other slice and cut in half.

Note: If you are watching your calories or cholesterol, you can just toast the bread dry with no butter. And before you top with bread, you can add a slice of bacon or 2 slices of avocado.

As an adult, my fallback recipe, ever since I can remember, has been Angel Hair spaghetti.

Billy's Angel Hair Pasta

Cook the spaghetti for 6 to 9 min
Toss it in Olive Oil
Add sautéed, diced garlic and Pecorino Romano Cheese.

That's it. Simple and elegant."

Leave it to Beaver

Leave It to Beaver delighted TV audiences with six seasons and 234 episodes, debuting on CBS on October 4, 1957, and running through June 20, 1963. It revolves around the boyhood of Theodore "The Beaver" Cleaver, played by Jerry Mathers and his family with Barbara Billingsley and Hugh Beaumont as Beaver's parents, June and Ward Cleaver, and Tony Dow as Beaver's big brother Wally.

The Cleavers eventually came to epitomize the perfect '50s suburban family. Despite the fact the show never won an award or made it into the top 30, *Leave It to Beaver* has achieved iconic status, arguably the most popular sitcom of the era.

Jerry Mathers

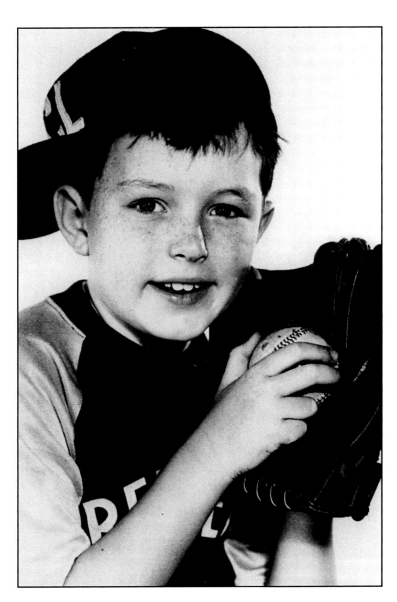

As Theodore "Beaver" Cleaver on the ever-popular sit-com *Leave It to Beaver*, Jerry Mathers won the hearts of viewers around the world when his well-intentioned antics nearly always led to mischief. From 1957 to 1963, the show has been seen in over 80 countries and translated into 40 languages.

"I can go anywhere in the world, and people know me," Mathers has said. "In Japan, the show's called *The Happy Boy and His Family*. So, I'll be walking through the airport in Japan, and people will come up and say, 'Hi, Happy Boy!'" Sixty-plus years later, it remains one of the longest-running scripted shows in TV history.

Jerry's television and show business career began at the tender age of two when he did a Pet Condensed Milk commercial with Ed Wynn on *the Colgate Comedy Hour*. He worked on many of the early '50's live television shows and, in 1954, made his movie in *This Is My Love*. His appearance in that film caught the attention of director Alfred Hitchcock who met with Jerry and signed him for the 1955 film, *The Trouble with Harry*, which starred John Forsythe and Shirley MacLaine in her first film role. That success was followed by two Bob Hope movies, *The Seven Little Foys*, *That Certain Feeling*, two films with Alan Ladd, *The Deep Six*, and *Men of the Fighting Lady*.

Jerry retired from acting as a teen to concentrate on his schooling. In 1966, while still in high school, he joined the United States Air Force Reserve. After graduation from in 1967, Jerry continued to serve in the Reserve and made the rank of Sergeant.

In 1982, Jerry rejoined most of his original TV family for a television movie, *Still the Beaver*. Its immense popularity led to the development of a new series, *The New Leave It to Beaver*, with Wally and the Beav, Eddie Haskell and Lumpy Rutherford all grown up with kids of their own. The show ran from 1983 to 1989, with Jerry moving behind the camera to direct several episodes.

In the mid- '90's Jerry was diagnosed with type 2 Diabetes. He took preventative action, lost 55 pounds, and is currently one of the leading lecturers on living and dealing with diabetes. Jerry has spoken to the Congressional Caucus on diabetes in Washington, DC and to various media outlets about the importance of early diagnosis, diet, and exercise. He also hosted a DVD on diabetic neuropathy, which is being distributed to patients at hospitals and free clinics across the country. Later, he became the national spokesperson for PhRMA and their Partnership for Prescription Assistance program, which helps uninsured and financially struggling patients obtain prescription medicines for free or nearly free.

In 2007, Jerry found new territory to conquer, making his Broadway debut starring as Wilbur Turnblad in the Tony Award-winning musical, *Hairspray*; and conquer he did, playing to standing room only houses with attendance at 110%.

Jerry Mathers continues to work in film and TV and to make personal appearances across the country. *People Magazine* has named him one of the most well-known individuals in television history.

"One of my favorite treats as a kid was the blueberry pie at Dupars restaurant in Studio City, California. It was across the street and down a block from Revue Studios, where we filmed the first two seasons of *Leave it to Beaver*. I would walk there with my mother for lunch, and always chose this restaurant when the press asked me to do a lunchtime interview."

Regrettably, this landmark eatery closed in January of 2018 after 70 years in business.

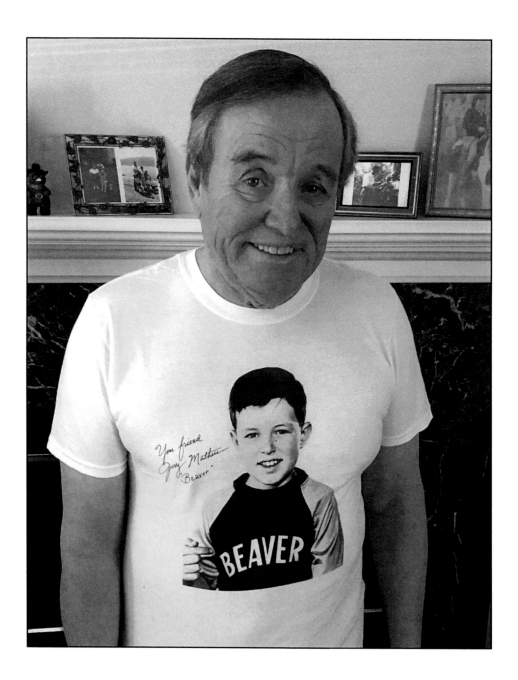

"As an adult, I faced some serious health issues and had to take a hard look at my diet. Fried food had to go, but the thought of no more fried chicken was terrible. So I searched until I came up with this:

Jerry Mathers Non-fried Fried Chicken

Ingredients:
- Cut up chicken parts (thighs, legs, breasts, wings)
- Panko bread crumbs
- Pinch dried rosemary
- Dash seasoned salt and pepper
- Olive Oil
- Garlic cloves
- Freshly squeezed lemon juice

Wash chicken and lightly coat with olive oil.
Dip the pieces into a bowl of Panko breadcrumbs
mixed with dried rosemary, and seasoned salt and pepper.
Coat all sides and place in a roasting pan lined with olive oil,
cut up garlic cloves and lemon juice.
Bake at 350 degrees for 1 hour

Enjoy the delicious taste of fried chicken with a healthy baked alternative! June Cleaver would be proud!"

Tony Dow

Even though Tony's mother was "IT" Girl, Clara Bow's double, a Mack Sennett bathing beauty and one of Hollywood's first stuntwomen, Muriel Montrose Dow had no aspirations for her son, Tony, to have a career in the entertainment industry. At an early age, he had earned many national swimming records and the reputation of the best junior diver in the country. In 1956, at age 11, his Olympic quest was interrupted when a long-time family friend asked if Tony could accompany him to the studio to meet with the producers for a new TV series, *Johnny Wildlife:* and he landed the part. The pilot never sold, but within a few months, Tony had to choose from the role of "Boy" in *Tarzan*, being a Mouseketeer, or playing the big brother on a sitcom. Fate helped him make the right decision. *Leave it to Beaver* was in production for 6 years and became one of America's all-time favorite sitcoms. The Cleavers and the town of Mayfield celebrated their 60th anniversary in 2017. Playing Wally Cleaver set the stage for Tony Dow's multi-faceted career in the field of entertainment.

After *Beaver,* Tony made guest appearances on shows like *Mr. Novak, My Three Sons, Dr. Kildare, The New Mike Hammer, Murder, She Wrote, Quincy, Knight Rider, Square Pegs, Love Boat*, and even played a cannibal on a two-part episode of *Freddy's Nightmares.* Tony co-starred in TV movies and was featured for several years on two daytime soaps *General Hospital* and *Never Too Young*, the latter being one of his favorite projects.

Tony soon moved behind the camera, where he enjoyed a 20-year career as a director. He loved the freedom the job afforded him; and was able to move from comedy to drama with ease, working on a variety of shows from *Coach* to *Star Trek: Deep Space 9*, and from *Honey, I Shrunk the Kids* to the award-winning *Babylon-5*. Other directing work includes: *Harry and the Hendersons, The New Lassie, Cover Me: The Real-Life Story of an FBI Family* and *The New Leave it to Beaver*, two episodes of which he also wrote.

As a producer, Tony, his wife, Lauren and Melissa Gilbert conceived the successful two-hour documentary *Child Stars: Their Story* for A&E. From kid stars, he segued to sci-fi, writing and producing a remake of the classic *It Came from Outer Space* for Universal, and producing and supervising visual effects for both *The Adventures of Captain Zoom in Outer Space* and for the movie/pilot, *Doctor Who* for Universal and the BBC.

Tony's hat rack just keeps getting bigger. He switched hats again to become a theater performer. In addition to doing *Love Letters* with Lauren, he has starred in stage productions of *Barefoot in the Park, Come Blow Your Horn, Lovers and Other Strangers* ,and the 17-month national tour of *So Long, Stanley.* Naturally, he couldn't help directing some theater as well; and received a *Dramalogue* award for directing the first West Coast production of *K-2.*

Tony now spends his time pursuing a life-long interest in sculpture. (Another hat, who's counting?) His work was recently chosen as one of two sculptors to represent the United States in an international exhibition at the Louvre in Paris.

Tony met and fell in love with the lovely Lauren while shooting a commercial for McDonald's. She was the producer who cast him in the role. Tony is endlessly proud of his son, Christopher, a City Firefighter in Fresno, where he lives with wife, Melissa and their twelve-year-old daughter, Tyla. That makes Tony a grandpa—his most favorite hat of all.

"My favorite recipe from kidhood was a concoction my mother made up when my brother, Dion, was young. It is the first thing I was able to prepare myself.

Tony's Breakfast Rice Cakes

 Scramble a couple of eggs in a large bowl with two cups of cold, cooked rice.
Prepare a frying pan with a generous amount of butter.
Dump the rice and egg mixture into the pan and flatten it out.
When starting to brown, turn over with a bit more butter in the pan.
When golden brown and crispy on both sides, put on plates and butter as you would toast.
Now the good part! Sprinkle the buttered rice cakes with powdered sugar and enjoy.
As you can see, it's not the healthiest of dishes—but the more butter and powdered sugar, the better.

Not recommended for people with clogged arteries!

I eat a lot healthier these days. This is one of my favorite salads for lunch or dinner.

Tony's Healthy Salad

Romaine, baby spinach, Bibb and iceberg lettuce
Crispy, uncured, smoked bacon cut into tiny bits with kitchen scissors
Cut large, not too ripe avocado into chunks
Blue cheese salad dressing. I love Trader Joe's, refrigerated.
Add: a touch of balsamic vinegar
1 hard-boiled egg grated on top of tossed salad
Extra, crumbled blue cheese
Coarse, black pepper ground

Lauren likes cherry tomatoes in her salad and sweet, hot jalapenos.
I prefer homemade croutons."

I Love Lucy

I Love Lucy is literally the mother of them all—the most popular sitcom in TV history. The show originally ran for six seasons on CBS from October 15, 1951 to May 6, 1957, with a total of 180 half-hour episodes. It starred Lucille Ball and her real-life husband Desi Arnaz as Lucy and Ricky Ricardo with Vivian Vance and William Frawley as Ethel and Fred Mertz, their best friends and landlords in their New York apartment building. Lucy portrays a dizzy redhead with the best of intentions who always seems to get in trouble, usually with one or both of the Mertzes. *I Love Lucy* became the most watched show in the United States in four of its six seasons; and has been syndicated in dozens of languages across the world.

When Lucy and Ricky had a baby, Little Ricky, the episode was the most watched TV show in history with 71.7% of America tuned in, surpassing the audience for President Eisenhower's inaugeration the next morning.

Keith Thibodeaux

Hailed as a child prodigy, Keith Thibodeaux started drumming at the age of 2 in Lafayette, Louisiana. By 3, he was making $500 a week on a national tour with the Horace Heidt Orchestra.

In 1955, Keith's dad took him to audition for the part of Little Ricky, son of Lucille Ball and Desi Arnaz on the number one show in America, *I Love Lucy*. Lucille Ball looked at the 5-year-old and said, "OK, he's cute; but what does he do?" Keith's dad told her he played the drums. "Oh, I can't believe that. We have a drum set over there, go ahead and play."

Needless to say, Keith blew her socks off. Desi came over and started jamming with him. After a minute, he stood up and said, 'Well, I think we found Little Ricky.'" Just like that, Keith was handed a starring role as Little Ricky Ricardo on *I Love Lucy show* and *The Lucy-Desi Comedy Hour*. Desi changed Keith's name to Richard Keith, which he felt was far easier than the Cajun French Thibodeaux. Keith got more than a great part; he became part of the family. He and Desi, Jr. became best friends. He went to Lucy and Desi's house on weekends and traveled with them and their children during the summer. "My mother kind of adopted him," said Lucie Arnaz. "He is in all our home movies and family photographs growing up." For a long time, Lucie thought they were actually related.

After the show ended in 1960, Keith guested on several popular shows, including *Route 66*, *The Shirley Temple Playhouse*, *Ben Casey*, *The Farmer's Daughter* and for four years, he played Opie's best friend on *The Andy Griffith Show*.

Keith with Ronny Howard

Then suddenly it was over. Keith's parents divorced, and he moved back to Louisiana with his mom. While attending the University of Louisiana in Lafayette, Keith joined and recorded with the then mainstream rock band, David and the Giants. But Keith had lost his way. He left the group after several years. His problems eventually led to solutions he found in the church and as a born-again Christian. Other members of the band followed. They regrouped under the same name and went on to become one of the nation's top contemporary Christian music groups. As a drummer, singer, and songwriter for the Dove-nominated group, Keith toured extensively for 10 years in the United States, Canada, Jamaica, and England, recording nine albums before leaving the group in 1989 to pursue other interests.

In 1976, Keith married Kathy Denton, a ballet dancer, in Jackson, Mississippi. After he left the band, Keith joined her on the road touring nationally and internationally with her company Ballet Magnificat! In 1993, Keith became the company's Executive Director. In 2017 the couple pioneered Ballet Magnificat! Brazil, a dance company and trainee program headquartered in Curitiba, Brazil. Keith and Kathy have one daughter, Tara, who is a dancer and choreographer.

In addition to his current responsibilities at Ballet Magnificat!, he also found time to write. His autobiography, *Life After Lucy*, was published in 1994 and tells the story of his life as

Little Ricky and his religious awakening. And Keith still makes time for his first love, the drums.

"As a kid at the studio, my go-to was hamburgers and chocolate sodas at the commissary on the Desilu Cahuenga lot where *I Love Lucy, Andy Griffith,* and *Dick Van Dyke* were filmed. When I was on *Andy Griffith,* Ron Howard and I would enjoy a hamburger and French fries next to Dick and Mary Tyler Moore sitting in the next booth!"

Keith's Chocolate Soda

3 tablespoons chocolate syrup
1 tablespoon half-and-half cream
3/4 cup carbonated water
1/4 cup vanilla ice cream

In a tall glass, combine chocolate syrup and cream. Stir in water; top with ice cream. Serve immediately.

Keith's French Toast

Beat 4 free range eggs and add a little raw honey and a splash of whole organic milk. Dip bread in mixture, both sides. Add Coconut oil in the pan and cook on medium heat until just brown. Sometimes I'll put a dab of grass fed butter on top to finish.

Lassie: Jeff's Collie

Lassie follows the adventures of a beloved collie dog and her boy, Jeff, played by Tommy Rettig, living in a fictional American farm town with Jeff's widowed mother, Ellen (Jan Clayton) and her father-in-law, Gramps (George Cleveland).

Jeff's best friend, Sylvester "Porky" Brockway was played by Joey Vieira who used the professional name Donald Keeler. Porky and his basset hound, Pokey, filled out the rest of the regulars. This first version of the series ran on CBS for 116 episodes from September 12, 1954 until December 1, 1957. Later it was syndicated as *Jeff's Collie*.

Joey D. Vieira

Joey D. Vieira recently celebrated his 65th year in show business. As a child, he co-starred in the first version of *Lassie* to come to television using the name Donald Keeler (Keeler for his famous auntie, tap dancing actress Ruby Keeler.) The show won two Emmy Awards between 1954 and 1958. The four years of the long-running series with Tommy Rettig as Jeff and his best pal, Porky are still entertaining audiences today.

Joey made appearances on other top television series, including *Dobie Gillis*, *My Three Sons*, and *Hank*. He starred in live television dramas like *Playhouse 90*, *Shirley Temple Storybook*, *The George Gobel Show* and a special with legendary Bob Hope. In 1955, he made the first of 21 feature films when he co-starred with Charlton Heston in *The Private War of Major Benson*. Other memorable films include *Ferris Bueller's Day Off, Red Heat,* and *The Patriot* as Peter Howard in which he starred with Mel Gibson.

Joey has a diverse background in other areas of the business as well. He has produced several recording artists, including Rick Springfield and Taylor Dane, and has written memorable jingles for national TV commercials, including Miller Beer

and Windsong Perfume. He's produced and directed national television and radio commercials for such heavyweights at AT&T, Ford, Subaru, Northern Telecom, and Mattel Toys.

As a writer, Joey co-created the 3-hour musical variety special for NBC, *Motown Returns to the Apollo Theater,* which won an Emmy for Best Variety Special of the Year. He also directed presentation videos for some of the top corporations in the world.

Recently, Joey has been working primarily in voice-overs for TV and DVD. He hopes the next 50 years in the biz will be at least half as exciting and rewarding as the first half-century has been.

"My favorite food as a kid–let me correct that–the only food provided for the cast and crew on the set in the 1950s was DOUGHNUTS with milk and coffee.

As for my favorite recipe today, I believe that whether you are having beef, chicken, pasta, pork, Chinese, Thai, fish, or any other entrée, a salad is the most complementary addition to enhance your meal. For my recipe, I am going to share with you the ingredients of a salad that is not only delicious but very healthy. I also include four salad dressings that cover all of the above main dishes.

Joey's Salad for Two

Cut off the knob of a bunch of romaine lettuce.
Tear the majority of leafy lettuce off.
This leaves you with the center of the leaf—the hearts of romaine.
Wash well under cold water and lay on paper towel.
Pat the water away. Chop lettuce on a wooden cutting board and place in a large bowl.

Slice one large tomato. Remove white center part.
Cut tomato into small sections, lightly salt and pepper and add it to the bowl.

Skin an avocado, remove pit and cut into small cubes.
Lightly salt and pepper and add to the bowl.

Use plenty of cucumber. Cut both ends off the part you are preparing.
Place one end of cucumber on wooden cutting board, push down hard and make circles until the inside of the cucumber is tender.
Repeat with the other end.
With peeler, remove skin and cut into thin slices.
Lightly salt and add to bowl.

Croutons are optional. If you use them, make sure they are small and few so as not to turn your salad into garlic cheese toast.

Dressings:

I have four dressings that compliment this salad while allowing for a variety of entrees.
Two are store-bought:
Ken's Steak House Italian with aged Romano cheese.
Kraft's Creamy Cucumber Ranch

I make my own 1000 Island

Joey's 1000 Island Dressing

In bowl, mix 75% mayo and 25% ketchup.
Put 2 tablespoons of sweet pickle relish onto paper towel to drain the juice.
Put relish in bowl.
Add one finely chopped hard-boiled egg.
Lightly salt and pepper.

I also make my own Asian dressing:

Joey's Own Asian Dressing

In a bowl, mix 65% Italian dressing with 35% "Soy Vay" Toasted Sesame dressing.
Salt and pepper to taste.
Mix well and chill."

The Mickey Mouse Club

The Mickey Mouse Club, created by Walt Disney, was first televised for four seasons, from 1955 to 1959, by ABC. An amazingly talented group of teens called Mouseketeers joined host Jimmie Dodd and "Big Mouseketeer," Roy Williams, for a variety show—singing and dancing between cartoons, dramatic serials and in-studio comedy.

Annette Funicello is a face most often associated with the original *Mickey Mouse Club*. She and many of the young people from the show went on to have exciting careers beyond the ears.

Annette Funicello

If Classic TV kids have a queen, it is Annette Funicello, though all you have to say is Annette for Baby Boomers to know exactly who you mean. "America's Sweetheart" was born in New York in 1942, but moved to Los Angeles at the age of four. A shy child, Annette's mother enrolled her in dance class to help her overcome it. Bingo! It was love at first plie. ˊ She dreamed of being a ballerina. When she danced the lead in "Swan Lake" at a recital in Burbank, Walt Disney saw Annette for the first time; and asked her to audition for the Mouseketeers. In October 1955, she and 23 other multi-talented kids made their television debut on *The Mickey Mouse Club*. Wholesome, curvy, with girl-next-door beauty, Annette quickly became the most popular, receiving 10 times the fan mail of any of the others.

She was soon starring in her own serial titled *Annette*. In one episode, she sang "How Will I Know My Love?" and the fan reaction was so enthusiastic, Disney released it as a single. "Uncle Walt" then put the renowned Sherman Brothers to work writing pop hits for her like "Tall Paul" and "Pineapple Princess." Annette went on to record 15 albums for Disney.

Annette remained at Disney when the Mouseketeers ended in 1959, starring in films like *The Shaggy Dog*, *Babes in Toyland* and *The Misadventures of Merlin Jones* with Tommy Kirk; and in TV serials like *Zorro*.

An invitation from *American Bandstand* host Dick Clark to tour with his "Caravan of Stars" led to a brief romance with recording idol Paul Anka. Walt Disney disapproved and nipped it in the bud, telling her it was nothing but puppy love. Anka wrote one of his biggest early hits about their short-lived relationship, "Puppy Love."

Next came *Beach Party* co-starring Frankie Avalon for American International Pictures. One of the first companies to cater to the burgeoning teen market, they featured bikini babes, surfers and rock and roll. What could go wrong? The movie was a smash and created its own genre. AIP used the formula to produce a string of the successful romp coms with Annette.

In between films, she guested on TV series like *Wagon Train*, *Burke's Law* and *The Greatest Show on Earth*. She and Tommy Kirk made a sequel to *Merlin Jones* called *The The Monkey's Uncle* in which she sang with the Beach Boys. Young people went to the theaters in droves to see it.

She married Paul Anka's agent, Jack Gilardi, in 1965. The couple had three children, and Annette devoted herself to them. She continued to appear on talk shows and as a guest on various TV series like *Love, American Style*, *Fantasy Island*, *The Love Boat*. She had a short role in the Monkees film *Head*.

Motherhood did not detract from Annette's relevance in the industry; in fact, it enhanced it. In 1979, she became the spokesperson for Skippy Peanut Butter, appearing in commercials with her real-life kids. Annette and Gilardi divorced in 1983. Three years later, she married Glen Holt, a harness racing horse trainer. The following year, Annette reunited with Frankie Avalon for the film *Back to the Beach* and a concert tour to promote it.

On the tour, she suffered bouts of dizziness and had some difficulty walking. Soon after, she was diagnosed with multiple sclerosis. She hid her condition for years until one day in 1992

when she overheard someone whisper that she must be drunk. She knew then she had to go public.

She created the Annette Funicello Fund for Neurological Disorders at the California Community Foundation, which raises funds for research in the search for a cure. Even as the degenerative disease took its toll, Annette spoke nationwide, educating people about MS…until she no longer could. Eventually, it robbed her of her ability to walk, to speak, to move. Twenty-five years after her diagnosis, Annette died from it in April 2013. She was 70. The news of her death marked an extraordinary outpouring of sadness from friends and fans.

"We are so sorry to lose Mother," her children said in a statement. "She is no longer suffering anymore and is now dancing in heaven."

Bob Iger, Chairman, and CEO of the Walt Disney Company, remembered her this way:

Annette was and always will be a cherished member of the Disney family, synonymous with the word Mouseketeer, and a true Disney Legend. She will forever hold a place in our hearts as one of Walt Disney's brightest stars, delighting an entire generation of baby boomers with her jubilant personality and endless talent. Annette was well known for being as beautiful inside as she was on the outside, and she faced her physical challenges with dignity, bravery and grace. All of us at Disney join with family, friends and fans around the world in celebrating her extraordinary life.

As the spokeswoman for Skippy Peanut Butter, naturally, Annette had a peanut butter recipe.

Annette Funicello's Peanut Butter Chocolate Chip Cookies

(Makes 2 to 3 dozen)

2 cups unsifted flour
1 cup granulated sugar
1/2 teaspoon baking soda
2 eggs
1/4 teaspoon salt
1 tablespoon water
1/2 cup corn oil margarine, softened
1 teaspoon vanilla extract
6 ounces semisweet chocolate chips
1/2 cup creamy or chunky peanut butter

Heat oven to 375 degrees F.
In small bowl stir together flour, sugar, baking soda and salt.

In large bowl with mixer at low speed, beat together margarine, peanut butter, eggs, water and vanilla extract just until blended.
Add flour mixture,
Beat until blended.
Increase speed to medium; beat 2 minutes.
Stir chocolate pieces into batter.
Drop by rounded tablespoonsful 3 inches apart onto ungreased cookie sheets.
Flatten slightly with floured bottom of glass.
Bake for 10 to 12 minutes or until lightly browned.
Cool on wire rack.
 Store in tightly covered container.

Annette Funicello's Steak in a Bag

(6 servings)

2 pounds top sirloin steak, cut 2 1/2 inches thick
2 tablespoons garlic spread
2 tablespoons vegetable oil
1 teaspoon salt
1 1/2 teaspoons seasoned pepper
1/2 cup Cheddar cheese, shredded
1 cup bread crumbs

Trim fat from steak. Make a paste from garlic spread, vegetable oil, salt and seasoned pepper.
Spread on both sides of steak.

Combine cheese and bread crumbs; pat on steak. Place steak in brown paper bag (large enough to fit steak comfortably).
Seal loosely with paper clips.
Bake in preheated 375 degrees F. oven for 30 minutes.
Increase oven temperature to 425 degrees F. and bake steak for 15 minutes longer.
Unseal bag to serve.

For easy handling, place bag on cookie sheet during baking. Annette advises, "You can bake steak early in the day, then bake at 425 degrees F. just before serving. The steak is out of this world."

Sharon Baird

Everyone has something inside, and Sharon Baird has dance inside of her. Ballet, Jazz, tap— she could do it all. Not only was she loaded with talent, but her tiny size made her look much younger, making her seem even more remarkable.

In 1950, Sharon, 7, won a "Little Miss Washington" contest in her hometown of Seattle. The prize was a trip to Los Angeles to compete in the national pageant. She won second place… and a new home. Her parents decided to move there. Sharon's life would forever change because of it. Almost immediately, she began studying tap with renowned dancer Louis Da Pron who sent her to audition for a skit on *The Colgate Comedy Hour*. She didn't get the part, but the show's host, Eddie Cantor, put her under personal contract. Whenever he hosted the show, he put her in it; but Cantor suffered a heart attack two years later and worked dropped off considerably.

Then Fate played its hand. While at a recording session at Capitol Records, Sharon was spotted by Jimmie Dodd, one of the co-hosts of Disney's upcoming show *The Mickey Mouse Club*. He insisted she audition for it. Not only did she get the job, she was featured in almost every show the first year.

Sharon's talents continued to grow—but Sharon didn't. Her diminutive size, which had worked in her favor as a child now worked against her as a teen. Most of the boys towered over her, and she looked more like Annette's kid sister than her peer. She found herself with less and less to do on the show. When it ended in 1958, Sharon performed at Disneyland with some of the other Mouseketeers. More importantly, she finished her education. At Los Angeles Valley College, she was president of the class of '63 and made the National Honor Society.

In the 1970s, Sharon found a job beautifully suited to her talents AND her size working on children's shows conceived by the brilliant Sid and Marty Krofft. Sharon appeared in elaborate costumes in shows like *H.R. Pufnstuf*, *The Bugaloos*, *Sigmund and the Sea Monsters* and *Land of the Lost*.

She added live-action modeling to her resume when she worked for the renown animator, Ralph Bakshi. She modeled for the role of Frodo Baggins in Bakshi's *Lord of the Rings*.

In 1980, Disney invited Sharon and her fellow Mouseketeers to appear in a television special for *The Wonderful World of Disney*, She even got to perform her famous tap-dance while jumping-rope routine. For a many years afterward, she and other Disney stars thrilled crowds in live shows on weekends at Disneyland. In 1984, Baird toured with comedian, Gallagher, performing a tap routine and aiding him in his sledge hammer-to-water melon routine. In 1986, she had the lead role in Sondra Locke's misguided film *Ratboy*.

Sharon now lives in semi-retirement in Reno, Nevada. She continues to make personal appearances with her lifetime friends, the other Mouseketeers, and Disney stars with whom she worked. She was devastated by the loss of her dear friend, Annette, from MS in 2013. Sharon remains in the hearts of her many fans from those years as well as the Kroft years. She continues to be a popular guest at nostalgia conventions nationwide.

"Annette and I were great friends. We had lunch together almost every day at the Disney Commissary. Our favorite thing was to get the bones from the prime rib they were serving to the executives in their private dining room. You could get the bones for about a quarter a piece and they were delicious. We loved them. But the executives got wind of what we were doing and adios to the bones! I guess they kept them for themselves. Annette and I were devastated!

At home, Mom overcooked everything. Dad was one of 10 kids and learned to cook dishes that went a long way for a little money…like his rice dish.

Mr. Baird's Rice Dish with Meat

1 lb hamburger meat
1 onion chopped
1 cup cooked rice
1/3 cup of bell pepper chopped

Combine ingredients in a pan and lightly brown.
Add:

2 cans tomato sauce
2 cans water

Simmer 10 minutes, then add:

1 tsp of mustard
Italian seasoning if desired

And that's it! I still make this in the winter in Reno when it's snowy. The older I get, the easier things get, the better I like it. Crock pots are great for that. In fact, here is the easiest thing I make.

Sharon's Easiest Dish

Place a pork butt in a crock pot. Pour 1 can of Nathan's sauerkraut over it. Cover and cook. That's it.

But my favorite as an adult is a recipe given to me by a friend.

Sharon's Borrowed Recipe for 10 Can Chili

In a crock pot:
- 1 lb ground beef – browned and drained
- 1 lb bulk sausage – browned and drained
- 1 whole onion chopped
- 1 7 oz can chopped green chilis
- 1 can hominy
- 1 can garbanzo beans (drained)
- 1 can kidney beans
- 1 can black beans
- 1 can Navy beans
- 1 can Pinto beans
- 1 can of white or red beans
- 1 can diced tomatoes with garlic and onions
- 1 can diced tomatoes chili ready
- 1 packet (dry) of taco seasoning
- 1 packet (dry) of Hidden Valley Ranch dressing

You can substitute the beef and sausage for turkey. When thoroughly heated, it's ready. Serve with corn bread; or crumble tortilla chips on top. (I use Fritos.)"

The Adventures of
Spin and Marty

Spin and Marty, a serial shown as part of *The Mickey Mouse Club*, starred David Stollery as Martin "Marty" Markham, a rich orphan, and Tim Considine as Spin Evans, poor, but the most popular boy at the Triple R Ranch, a Western-style summer camp. They instantly dislike one another but end up best pals. It ran from 1955 through 1957 for a total of 78 11-minute episodes.

Tim Considine and David Stollery

Tim Considine and David Stollery have been friends since they first met on the set of an MGM Greer Garson film called *Her Twelve Men* in 1954. But for fans of *The Mickey Mouse Club*, they are forever linked as Spin and Marty, from the show's most popular serial, *The Adventures of Spin and Marty*.

Tim Considine's family was steeped in show business on both sides. Dad was an Oscar-nominated producer, and his mother's father was theater magnate Alexander Pantages.

Early on, Tim made his own decision to be an actor; and his very first role was starring opposite master comedian Red Skelton in *The Clown*, a remake of *The Champ*. The drama culminates in a tear-jerking dramatic climax with Tim near hysterics – not for the inexperienced actor much less a 13-year-old boy who'd never been in front of a camera before. Yet Tim carried it off beautifully. The kid was great. "Skelton helped me a lot," is all he'll say about it.

That same year he made his television debut on an episode of *Ford Television Theatre* in another highly dramatic starring role. Offers for work were plentiful, among them: *Executive Suite, The Private War of Major Benson,* and TV's *The Adventures of Rin-Tin-Tin.*

In 1955, Disney asked Tim to audition for the lead role of an orphaned rich kid, Martin Markham for a serial of the same name. It told the story of life on the Triple R Ranch, where boys got to enjoy the great outdoors, riding, camping, doing chores. Marty arrived in a chauffeur-driven limo with a manservant in tow. Tim was tired of playing that type of character. He wanted to play the hip kid, Spin Evans, who ends up clueing Marty in. Disney said yes and changed the name of the show to *The Adventures of Spin and Marty*. It quickly became *the Mickey Mouse Club's* most popular serial.

Tim also starred in other fan favorite serials: *The Hardy Boys* with Disney star Tommy Kirk and, along with David, in *Annette* with Miss Funicello.

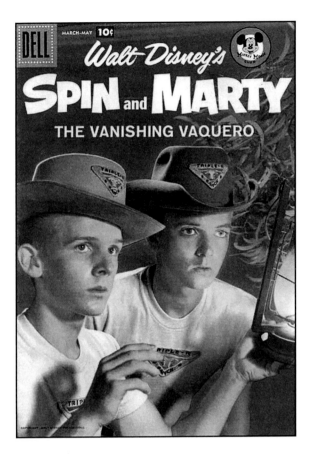

In 1959, as *the Mouse Club* came to an end, Tim guested in TV Western series *Zane Grey Theater, Cheyenne,* and *Johnny Ringo.* And with Fred MacMurray, Tommy Kirk, Annette, and loveable Kevin Corcoran, he starred in the Disney hit film, *The Shaggy Dog.*

At 19, Uncle Sam tapped Tim for a more important role in the US Air Force. With a heavy work schedule already set up, he was able to defer his military service while he made the film *Sunrise at Campobello*, an episode of *The Untouchables* and a TV pilot with Fred MacMurray about a widower with three sons. Tim played the eldest son Mike Douglas on *My Three Sons* from 1960 until 1965. A young man now, Tim longed to stretch his creative wings. He'd written one script for the show and directed a few scenes, but when he asked to do more, the producers refused; and Tim made the decision to leave the show. He continued performing on episodic television shows like *Bonanza, The Fugitive, Medical Center, Gunsmoke* and *Ironside* as well a memorable bit in the Oscar-winning film *Patton.*

In later years, Tim pursued writing, journalism and photography and a passion for fast cars. It carried him to his greatest role as an automobile historian, photographer, and writer specializing in auto racing. David Stollery also has an interest in fast cars. He and Tim share common interests and a deep friendship that has continued throughout their lives.

David Stollery was also born into a theatrical family. Both of his parents were in radio—his dad, an announcer, and his mom, an actress. When his mother's career ended, she pushed her son into the business. And work came easily for him. At age 7, he toured with the great Judith Anderson in *Medea*. And over the next three years, he appeared in five films, mostly uncredited, but the offers kept coming and the roles got larger until 1951 when he scored his first featured role in a Joan Fontaine vehicle titled *Darling, How Could You?*

1952 was a great year for David. He worked with comedy legends Abbott and Costello in the film *Jack and the Beanstalk,* an episode of TV's *Dragnet* and most memorably as one of two unruly twins in *I Love Lucy* who, after tying her up, end up in a talent contest with her singing "Ragtime Cowboy Joe." Next came Broadway for Dave in the role of Pud in a revival of *On Borrowed Time.* His performance won him a child actor of the year award, which led to more stage work and episodic television working with stars like Red Skelton, Ray Milland, and Marie Wilson.

In 1954, David landed a role in an MGM film starring Greer Garson and Robert Ryan, *Her Twelve Men*. The most noteworthy thing about it was that 13-year-old David met castmate Tim Considine, a boy who would become his life-long friend.

Tim Considine isn't sure, but he may have suggested Dave for the role of Marty Markham. Or it might have been Mouseketeer Lonnie Burr's mom. Regardless, David was invited to audition and won the part. The studio immediately arranged for six weeks of horsebackriding lessons for Dave, who felt more than ready by July when the cameras rolled.

Dave starred in other Disney films as well, and co-starred with Tim again in 1956 in *The Further Adventures of Spin and Marty* and in 1957 in *The New Adventures of Spin and Marty*. That same year, he was cast in the enviable role of Annette Funicello's love interest in the serial, *Annette*.

David was 16 when *The Mickey Mouse Club* ended in 1959. He'd been feeling it for some time, but it was then he decided to dance to his own drummer. Show business had been good to him, but he was done with it. With interest in design, he enrolled in the Art Center in Pasadena, California, and graduated with a bachelor's degree in Industrial Design. After working for several prestigious companies, Dave eventually founded his own: Industrial Design Research in Southern California.

He and Tim Considine are still great pals, see each other frequently, and reunited in front of the cameras in 2005 to shoot a bonus feature for the *Spin & Marty* DVD. In 2000, they made cameo appearances in *The New Adventures of Spin and Marty: Suspect Behavior,* a made-for-TV movie.

"I honestly don't remember having any favorite foods during my teens," says Dave. "However, when I was working in New York in *On Borrowed Time*, I was introduced to lobster and then ordered it as much as possible. I really didn't develop an appreciation for food until I went to Italy in 1961 and worked there for a year. Of course, when I was old enough to drive, I would cruise Bob's Big Boy, but it wasn't for the food.

"As an adult, I developed this recipe to alleviate potential cholesterol deficiency. Of particular concern was my friend Tim Considine's diet, which is normally far too healthy and boring. Consequently, I make these ribs for his birthday every year, secure in the knowledge he gets something with a little flavor."

"Once a year on New Year's Eve—my birthday—Stollery makes ribs for me," says Tim. "They are sensational… and one more reason our friendship has lasted so long."

Dave's Spare Ribs

Pork spareribs (any kind will do)
Dredge ribs in flour seasoned with salt and pepper
Put ribs in a baking pan with a little water (about ½ a cup). A disposable foil pan is recommended.
Some sliced onions on the ribs adds a lot of flavor.
Cover the pan with aluminum foil and bake at 325 degrees for a couple of hours.
Take the ribs out of the oven and cut into individual pieces.

Coat each rib with your favorite barbeque sauce mixed with a can of crushed pineapple. 1/2 x 1/2 pineapple to sauce is recommended.

Put the coated ribs back in the oven uncovered and bake at 325 degrees for another hour. Ready to serve!"

Tim adds, "I've always loved Pink's hotdogs—still a favorite, for sure. They started in 1939 and remain one of the few things in Hollywood older than I am!"

Wagon Train

This popular Western attracted big-name guest stars who joined the regulars as the wagon train made its arduous journey from Missouri to California every week, led by wagon master Ward Bond. After his death, John McIntire and Robert Horton came on board, later replaced by Scott Miller and Robert Fuller. The series ran for eight seasons from 1957 to 1965 with 284 episodes, reaching the number one slot in the ratings for a time.

Lou Costello made a rare dramatic appearance on the series.

Beverly Washburn

A story from a 1957 *TV Guide*, headlined "For Crying Out Loud," focuses on Beverly Washburn's claim to fame: an uncanny ability to cry on cue. Anyone who's ever seen the 1957 Disney classic *Old Yeller* can testify to Washburn's ability to turn on the tears. "My brother used to say I could cry at a supermarket opening," she chuckles.

Actor Jock Mahoney, TV's *Range Rider* and *Yancey Derringer*, was very taken with Beverly at a benefit performance. The chance meeting led to 6-year-old Beverly's big break. Six months later, at a Columbia Pictures audition, Mahoney, remembered Beverly and put in a word for her. She got the part.

That debut role—as a little girl who dies of smallpox in 1950s *The Killer That Stalked New York* led to Frank Capra's *Here Comes the Groom,* then Cecil B. DeMille's 1952 Oscar-winning *The Greatest Show on Earth* in which Washburn shared the screen with Jimmy Stewart. Danny Kaye sang "Thumbelina" to her in 1952's *Hans Christian Andersen.* And the next year, Washburn played a pioneer girl in George Stevens' classic Western, *Shane.* In fact, before Beverly Washburn turned 20, she had appeared in more than 500 films and TV shows, from *Fury, Zane Grey Theater* to *Gidget, Leave It to Beaver,* and *The Patty Duke Show.*

Beverly worked with Hollywood legends like Bing Crosby, Loretta Young, Barbara Stanwyck, Jack Benny, Kirk Douglas, and later Michael Douglas. She worked with the iconic Clayton Moore in *The Lone Ranger* and with superhero George Reeves in *Superman and the Mole Men*. She also co-starred with Lou Costello, half of the famous comedy team of Abbott and Costello of "Who's on First?" fame in the only dramatic role of his career in a memorable episode of *Wagon Train*. And she appeared in over 60 commercials.

Beverly now lives in Las Vegas and continues to work. She recently penned her autobiography, *Reel Tears*. Looking back on her long career, Ms. Washburn says she feels very, very blessed.

But as for her diet, she says, "I don't know how we survived! My parents

were from the Midwest and really brought that sensibility with them. Even though fresh food was all around us in Los Angeles, we never had salads. All our vegetables came from a can. Mom, as sweet as she was—cooking was not her long suit. Tuna casserole, mac and cheese…

Mom had a real sweet tooth, and I guess I inherited that from her. We lived in Hollywood on Fuller Avenue between Sunset Boulevard and Hollywood. My favorite treat was just a few blocks away at C.C. Brown's, 7007 Hollywood Boulevard, just half a block from Grauman's Chinese Theater. You could see anyone there—tourists to movie stars. It was like an old-fashioned ice cream parlor inside. I loved the big, high-back wooden booths and the heavy wooden tables. My best friend and I used to walk there; and I would always order the same thing: a Swiss chocolate sundae with almonds on top."

C.C. Brown's was a Hollywood landmark. Candymaker Clarence Clifton Brown brought copper kettles out west in a covered wagon from Ohio to Los Angeles in 1906. For 90 years, his hot fudge sauce was made in those same copper kettles. People lucky enough to have tasted a C. C. Brown's hot fudge sundae agree that no other could compare. Sadly, it closed its doors in 1996.

C.C. Brown's Hot Fudge Sundae

C.C. Brown's always made its classic sundae with French vanilla ice cream, warm, hand-chopped roasted almonds, and real home-made whipping cream, and served it in a silver goblet with the Hot Fudge Sauce in a small pitcher on the side.

1960s

In the progressive '60s, television began to reflect current social issues and the quickly changing times. By 1967, all three channels broadcast primetime in color. There was a move away from more traditional families to single-parent homes, as in *Family Affair* and *My Three Sons*. *The Monroes* had no parents at all; while Timmy from *Lassie* may have been the first adopted child in a series. Though the look of the family changed, the message remained the same. Even the escapist adventures of *Daniel Boone* and *The Munsters* had family values at their core. Space travel and the nuclear age loomed large.

Shows like *Lost in Space* and *The Twilight Zone* grabbed a new audience. Even the most light-hearted of family sitcoms like *The Dick Van Dyke Show* and *The Patty Duke Show* sometimes dealt with issues like racism and women's rights. By the end of the decade, *Julia* blazed a trail as the first TV show to star a black actress as something other than a maid or servant.

Daniel Boone

Daniel Boone starred Fess Parker as the American hero of this 1700s adventure series.

Wife Rebecca was played by Patricia Blair and children Jemima and Israel were played by Veronica Cartwright and Darby Hinton. Ed Ames portrayed Boone's companion, an Oxford-educated half-British Native American.

Set in the 1770s and 1780s, it ran from September 24, 1964, to May 7, 1970, on NBC for 165 episodes.

Veronica Cartwright

Veronica was born in Bristol, England, and emigrated to the United States as a young girl with her parents and sister Angela. She began her career modeling and doing print ads; and became the "Kellogg's Girl" doing commercials for Kellogg's Corn Flakes, Sugar Smacks, and Rice Krispies. At the age of 9, Veronica appeared in In *Love and War,* playing Robert Wagner's sister. She followed that with a semi-regular role on the CBS series, *Leave It to Beaver* as Violet Rutherford, famed for giving Beaver his first kiss. Other shows followed, such as *The Eleventh Hour, Alfred Hitchcock Presents,* and the classic episode of *The Twilight Zone* called *I Sing the Body Electric* as young Anne. There were many guest appearances on various shows and then the NBC serial, *Daniel Boone,* in which she played Jemima Boone from 1964 to 1966.

Her film career began in the classic films *The Children's Hour* directed by William Wyler, Alfred Hitchcock's *The Birds,* and in *Spencer's Mountain.*

Mrs. Cartwright and her girls

She made her transition into adult roles in such films as *Inserts* with Richard Dreyfuss and *Goin' South*, the first of three films in which she starred opposite Jack Nicholson. Veronica appeared in two science fiction classics in the 1970s, Philip Kaufman's remake of *Invasion of the Body Snatchers* and Ridley Scott's masterpiece thriller, *Alien*.

Veronica starred as Betty Grissom in the epic *The Right Stuff*. She made an indelible impression on movie-goers in 1987 with her standout performance in *The Witches of Eastwick*. She has appeared in over 50 movies.

She has also appeared in over 100 television movies and series, including *The Rat Pack*, *My Brother's Keeper*, and *RFK: His Life and Times* in which she played Ethel Kennedy. She also had a memorable recurring television role as the zealous prosecutor, Margaret Flanagan on *L.A. Law*.

Veronica has been nominated 4 times for an Emmy Award with one win. At age 15, she won an Emmy for Best Actress in a television movie called *Tell Me Not in Mournful Numbers*. She was nominated again in 1997 for her guest-starring role of Mrs. Huston in two widely acclaimed episodes of *ER*. In 1998 and 1999, the Television Academy nominated her twice for her pivotal role of Cassandra Spender on Fox's *The X Files*. She has guest-starred on television in *Criminal Minds*, *CSI Cyber*, *Grey's Anatomy*, *Will & Grace* and many other hit shows. Her many theatre credits from New York to Los Angeles resulted in brilliant reviews and three *DramaLogue* Awards for Best Actress. Veronica celebrates nearly 67 years in show business this year with many more to go for this remarkably versatile actress.

"My mom was not an accomplished cook unless you call putting a 6-pound eye of the round for Sunday dinner in at noon at 350 degrees and taking it out at 5:00—very dry. She complained every week how a 6-pound roast couldn't feed a family of four. Same for chicken breasts. Mom hated sauces as well so there was none of that. My dad always did the Thanksgiving turkey. That was great.

I did the cooking after school as Angela was working. We used to have set nights for dinner and, if I'm not mistaken, Shephard's Pie was Wednesday. The ingredients were purchased on the weekend. Back then, Shephard's Pie was ground beef, onion, frozen peas and carrots, mashed potatoes and a gravy made from Bisto. Very much a comfort food. I now make Shephard's Pie with a bit more of a flare. It's yummy. Bon appetite!"

Veronica's Shephard's Pie with Flare

(serves 3-4)

Preheat oven to 350-425 degrees
>Use 1 pound ground beef 85/15
>1 white onion
>Fresh carrots—about 6—cut into rounds-boil till tender but not soft. I use no salt.
>Fresh English Peas which you can get at Trader Joe's. Use about a 1/2 packet.
>Drop into water after carrots.
>3-4 Russet Potatoes, peeled, cut and boiled in salted water

The beef should be cooked, I use a cast iron pan, Salt and pepper to taste with 1 onion chopped fine. I add red pepper flakes and Herb de Provence.
Cook till done through.Mash the potatoes. I use heavy cream as there are no carbs in cream.
Do not make the potatoes too whipped. Should be a nice solid mash.
Place meat, carrots and peas in a casserole dish or Pyrex 8x8
The famous Bisto gravy can be purchased in powder or granules from a British shop or World Market Cost Plus. I use about 1 1/2 to 2 cups. You want to cover the meat and veggies.Place the mashed spuds on top of the meat mixture. I level them out and use a fork to make little channels.
You can put a little cream on top to brown or use fine ground Parmesan cheese.
Place tin foil under dish as it can bubble over. The top should be a bit crisp.
If need be put under broiler for a couple minutes.
Add A-1 Sauce if you'd like.

The Dick Van Dyke Show

The Dick Van Dyke Show, created by Carl Reiner, centered on the work and home life of television comedy writer Rob Petrie. It starred Dick Van Dyke with Mary Tyler Moore as wife, Laura and Larry Mathews as son Ritchie. Rob was head writer for the *Alan Brady Show* with co-writers Sally Rogers (Rose Marie) and Buddy Sorrell (Morey Amsterdam) who lived to insult the producer, Mel Cooley (Richard Deacon). Reiner played Brady. Supporting cast included next door neighbors Jerry and Millie Helper (Jerry Paris and Ann Morgan Guilbert). It ran five seasons on CBS from October 3, 1961, to June 1, 1966 with a total of 158 half-hour episodes.

Larry Mathews

Larry was born in Burbank, California on August 15, 1955. As the sixth of seven children, he had his work cut out for him to get attention; and he rose to the occasion. By the time Larry was three, he was entertaining not only his family, but half the neighborhood as well. At four, he began acting lessons that quickly led to an interview with Carl Reiner for the role of Ritchie Petrie, Rob and Laura's adorable son.

The Dick Van Dyke Show ran for 5 years on CBS, 1961-1966., garnering numerous Emmys including Best Comedy Series of the '65-'66 season. The show's longevity is truly a tribute to the creators, writers, cast, and crew. It continues to entertain people around the world and is honored by exhibits both at the Smithsonian Institute and the Museum of Broadcasting.

After the final episode was shot in 1966, Larry returned to life as a"regular kid." He continued to act in local stage productions throughout high school and college at UCLA. After graduation, Larry returned to the entertainment business he loved, but this time behind the scenes in production and post-production. He'd always been fascinated by what went on behind the camera. He immersed himself in "the nuts and bolts" of making movies and TV. During his 40+ year career, he has held several positions, including assistant producer, editor, assistant director, and post-production supervisor.

Recently Larry assembled an award-winning team of post- production artists for Juice Worldwide Post Services, a state of the art post facility in Burbank, where he serves as Vice President of Sales. He still does voice-over work and is involved in numerous ventures outside the entertainment industry.

Larry and Jennifer married in 1987 and recently moved back to Burbank, where it all began for him. Jen fully embraces Larry's Italian heritage, and the two travel frequently to Italy. They plan to live there one day. "I've had a great life," Larry says, "and it's only getting better. I wouldn't trade it for anything."

No surprise Larry's favorite dish as a kid is something Italian. "My mom made stuffed artichokes from a recipe she got from my Sicilian Grandmother… amazing.

Larry's Grandmother's

Italian Stuffed Artichokes

Take large artichoke.
Cut off the stems and the tips of the leaves.
Cut the stems into little pieces.
Mix up breadcrumbs, parmesan cheese, fresh diced garlic (garlic powder can be substituted) in a bowl.
Spread the artichoke leaves and stuff generously with breadcrumb mix.
Pour extra virgin olive oil lightly over the top so as to compact the stuffing.

In a Dutch oven or large pot, boil about 2 to 3 inches of water. Place the artichoke on a grate so you can steam it. Steam for 1 to 1½ hours, (depends on the size of the choke) adding water as needed so as not to burn the pot.

Test by pulling out a leaf. When leaf comes out easily, remove artichokes and enjoy… preferably with a good Italian red wine!

As for my favorite recipe as an adult, hands down, it's:

Larry's Marinated Grilled Halibut

Take one—or as many as needed — pieces of Halibut steak. (You can substitute any firm fish, ie swordfish, tuna etc.) Place in glass baking dish. Marinate with the following ingredients in order, portions to taste.

Dry White wine. Important you do not use sweet wine.
Fresh squeezed lemon juice
Small amount of Worcestershire sauce
Extra Virgin Olive Oil
Garlic Powder—generous portion
Black Pepper. From grinder is preferred

Flip fish over and repeat on other side. Cover with clear wrap and place in fridge.
Let marinate from 1 to 3 hours.

Heat grill up to medium heat. Take a large piece of aluminum foil and place on grill once temperature is ready.
Place fish on the foil for 5 to 8 minutes, depending on thickness of fish.
Brush or spoon marinade onto fish while cooking. Flip fish over and repeat procedure.
Remove from grill and serve with rice pilaf or any other desired grain dish.

Enjoy with dry white wine of choice, ie: Sauvignon Blanc, Chardonnay. If red wine is pre-ferred, have a Pinot Noir. Have Fun!"

Family Affair

Family Affair starred Brian Keith as Bill Davis, a successful engineer and bachelor living in a New York luxury apartment with his valet, Mr. French portrayed by Sebastian Cabot.

His lavish lifestyle is interrupted when, shortly after the death of Davis's brother and his wife, their three children come to live with him: 15-year old Cissy played by Kathy Garver, and five-year old twins Buffy and Jody played by Anissa Jones and Johnny Whitaker.

The series ran on CBS for five seasons from September 12, 1966, to March 4, 1971 and 138 episodes.

Kathy Garver

Most fondly remembered for her starring role as Cissy in the CBS television hit, *Family Affair*, Kathy Garver has also garnered critical acclaim in movies, stage, radio, voice-over animation, and audiobook narration.

Kathy was born in Long Beach, California, and began working professionally at the age of seven. Her first film, *The Night of the Hunter,* was directed by Academy Award winner Charles Laughton. The following year, Hollywood's legendary director, Cecil B. DeMille recognized Kathy's distinct talents on the set of *The Ten Commandments.* Initially hired for a small part in the epic motion picture, Kathy was noticed by the great director who added scenes to highlight the little girl.

During her teenage years, Kathy added radio and stage to her burgeoning film and television career. She was a freshman majoring in speech at UCLA when she tested for *Family Affair.* Kathy won the role of Cissy and co-starred for five years with Brian Keith, Sebastian Cabot, Anissa Jones, and Johnny Whitaker in one of the warmest sitcoms of the 1960s and 70s. The show's popularity continues to this day.

After *Family Affair*, Kathy starred in an Israeli musical stage version of the TV series, learning Hebrew phonetically for her role. Later, she continued her dramatic studies at London's prestigious Royal Academy of Dramatic Art. Dramatic and comedic productions in the states followed. Then she returned to UCLA to earn a Master's Degree in Theater Arts.

A versatile actress, her talents include vocal characterizations for cartoons, commercials, toys, and audiobooks. She even produced, narrated and wrote lyrics and original music for eight audio Beatrix Potter tales, which have sold over two million copies and have won numerous awards.

Having served on the board of the Young People's Committee of the Screen Actors Guild, Kathy has used her experience to help guide new actors in the business. She appears at gatherings, luncheons, and conventions to give motivational speeches, using her wealth of experience, and education to entertain and instruct people with her exciting and successful interactive speeches and presentations. From Keynote speaker to host to workshop leader, Kathy has enriched the lives of those who have been able to listen and learn from her inspirational communications.   Kathy enjoys her own "family affair." She met her husband

of 34 years, David Travis, on a tennis court in Palm Springs – truly a love match. They have one son, Reid.

"As a child, I liked tapioca pudding best. I found it a real comfort food. I remember once after my mom had cooked a great dinner and totally cleaned up the kitchen, her "little cherub" came into the sparkling kitchen and pleaded and begged for her most favorite dessert to be made by her most favorite mother; and my loving mother complied.

Mom never gave me her recipe, but there are plenty of good ones out there. Just make sure you check the directions on the packaging. Different brands of tapioca call for different instructions—some small tapioca requires the pearls to soak overnight, others for just 5 minutes. It can be served warm or cold. And it's gluten-free!

As an adult, I enjoy making this recipe which was handed down through my family from my Grandmother Marie from Austria who lived to be 101 years old.

Kathy's Kucumbers

1 cucumber (adjust ingredients for each additional cucumber)
Salt
2 tbs white or apple cider vinegar
3 chopped scallions
1 tsp sugar

Slice the cucumber as thinly as possible.
Put slices in a bowl in layers and sprinkle each layer with salt.
Cover the bowl, and refrigerate for 2 to 4 hours. Some of the moisture will have drained out.
Wring out the remaining moisture and discard.
Add the vinegar, scallions, and sugar. Oil is not needed.
Black pepper or red pepper flakes may be added to make the dish spicy.

This dish is a wonderful accompaniment to duck with red cabbage or any meat and potatoes meal."

Guestward Ho

Guestward Ho! was based on a memoir by Barbara "Babs" Hooton, played by actress Joanne Dru, who tires of the New York rat race and moves her family to New Mexico. Husband Bill was played by Mark Miller and son Brook by Flip Mark.

In the series, the family buys a dude ranch sight-unseen which requires considerable more work than they anticipated. Also in the show was veteran character actor, J. Carrol Naish as a rather pessimistic Native American named Hawkeye. The series aired on ABC the 1960-1961 television season for 38 episodes.

Flip Mark

The New York talent agent was on the phone with a photographer who was offering some modeling work for a red-haired, freckle-faced boy when 7-year-old Philip Goldberg walked into the office for the first time with his mother. The agent looked up, covered the phone receiver, and asked his mother, "What's his name?"

"Philip Goldberg," his mom said.

"That won't work," the agent said. "Does he have a nickname?"

"Flip."

"That's good. Does he have a middle name?"

"Mark."

The agent uncovered the receiver and said, "I've got the perfect boy. His name is Flip Mark."

Flip got that very first job and a new name and never looked back. He appeared in ads for everything from Kellogg's cereals to Ohrbach's department store chain. And that led to a career on stage, screen, and television. Talk about being in the right place at the right time.

"I did print work for a number of years, interspersed with television commercials," he says. At that time, almost everything [on TV] was live, in New York. The commercials led to parts on TV shows, a Broadway revival of *Annie Get Your Gun,* and eventually a movie shot in Europe in 1956 called *The Journey*—a Cold War story starring Yul Brynner and Deborah Kerr. Flip's younger brother was played by another red-haired, freckle-faced boy named Ron Howard.

When he returned to New York, the agent suggested that Goldbergs move to Hollywood, where Flip could find much more work. They decided to go on a family vacation to visit Disneyland and test the waters. Flip got a part in *Please Don't Eat the Daisies* playing one of the sons of Doris Day and David Niven. He also appeared in five episodes of *Lassie* with Jon Provost, who became a life-long friend. But it was a role in a sketch opposite comedian Shelley Berman in the 1960 Emmy-winning TV special, *The Fabulous Fifties* that was the turning point.

"After that show, I had offers for six TV series," Flip says. "I was a hot commodity and was interviewed by a newspaper in New York. The interview was done at Sardi's (a famous showbiz gathering place). Suddenly, someone yells out, 'You, kid.' We looked, and it was Jackie Gleason. He said, 'You were terrific [on 'The Fabulous Fifties'].'" Gleason didn't recall that he'd worked with Flip several years earlier.

Before he was offered a TV series, Flip's parents were content with the cross-country commute from New York to Hollywood; but that would be impractical if he took a role in a weekly series. His father told him, "If this is really what you want to do, we'll sell the house in New York ... and we'll just move out there." And that's what they did.

Guestward Ho, about a New York family who relocates to rural New Mexico to open a dude ranch, was his first TV series.

His second series was *Fair Exchange*, about a pair of World War II buddies—one British, one American—who decide to exchange their teenage daughters across the pond for a year. Flip played Larry Walker, son of Eddie Foy Jr., who got into mischief with the exchanged British daughter, a young Judy Carne well before her stint on *Laugh-In* made "sock it to me" part of the vernacular.

All the while, Flip worked in other films, including his favorite, *Safe at Home*, which united the young sports fan with baseball legends Roger Maris and Mickey Mantle. On TV, he guested on top shows like *The Outer Limits, Have Gun Will Travel, The Andy Griffith Show, My Favorite Martian, The Jack Benny Show, Mr. Ed, The Lucy Show, The Patty Duke Show, My Three Sons,* and *The Fugitive.* He even learned to ride a motorcycle in Dean Martin's driveway for his role in *Marriage on the Rocks,* starring Martin, Frank Sinatra, and Deborah Kerr.

He continued commuting from coast-to-coast because there was still a good deal of commercial work for him in New York, working with "Mr. Wizard" (Don Herbert) and General Electric. From 1965-1966, Flip appeared as the first Steven Olson in the soap

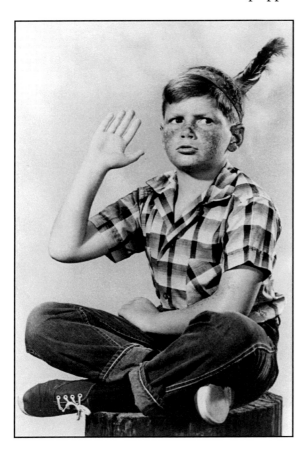

opera, *Days of Our Lives.* In 1968, he guest-starred in The Big Valley, with Barbara Stanwyck. His final screen roles were on *Mission: Impossible* and T*he Streets of San Francisco.* Then he was college-bound.

"It was an exciting time," Flip says. "In L.A., my mom came with me to the studio whenever I was working, and my dad did various things. I was contributing to the household and my dad made some real sacrifices for me to pursue that." And that meant some challenges. "It was a different world then. The money wasn't what it is now," he says; but overall, he recalls his parents' role in his unusual upbringing with fondness.

"They were unique among parents of child actors," he says. "Most directors and producers wanted nothing to do with stage parents. My parents were very grounded. They wanted me to be successful, but they wouldn't hesitate to say, 'He can't do an interview that day because he's got Cub Scouts or a Little League game.' Their attitude was, 'Don't get too full of yourself. We're not going to let that happen.' "

Flip followed his acting days with a career in the travel industry. He married and had a daughter, Jennifer, but lost his wife to cancer. The care he gave her led him to a nearly 20-year career working as a 9-1-1 operator. Years later, he married his high school sweetheart, Judy. "I've been fortunate. I've got three very defined stages of my life, each of them filled with excitement and some very good memories."

Flip with Jon Provost, then and now

"We filmed *Guestward Ho* at Desilu Studios in Culver City. In my childhood years, the extent of my culinary interest was defined by the Flip Mark burger at the studio commissary — a plain hamburger with ketchup. When you order the same boring thing every day, it just became easier for them to say, 'We need a Flip Mark burger.' Haute cuisine in my youth extended to that and not much more.

Here's a great recipe showing my evolution as an adult. The lemon chicken has always been a favorite of my wife, Judy; so it's become a staple around the house for guests.

Flip's Oriental Baked Chicken

(Serves 4-6)

½ cup of butter
¼ cup of honey
1 tbsp of soy sauce
¼ cup lemon juice
Flour, salt & pepper to coat pieces

Coat each chicken piece with flour mixture.
Melt ¼ cup of butter in pan.
Place each piece of chicken (skin side down) in pan and bake in oven for 30 minutes @ 350 degrees.
Meanwhile melt remainder of butter, all of honey & lemon juice and soy sauce in small bowl.
Place this cooked mixture in pan with overturned chicken pieces and continue cooking until golden brown, approximately 30 minutes, basting frequently.

Julia

Julia was the first weekly series since *Amos 'n' Andy* in which a black person who wasn't a maid or servant played the lead role.

The show starred actress/singer Diahann Carroll as widow, Julia Baker (her husband had been shot down in Vietnam), left to raise her young son, Corey, played by Marc Copage. Baker, a nurse, lands a job with a Caucasian doctor in the aerospace industry. The crusty but kind Dr. Morton Chegley was played by Lloyd Nolan. The then-controversial series ran three seasons and 86 episodes on NBC from September 17, 1968 to March 23, 1971.

Marc Copage

In 1968, when Julia premiered, Marc was a 5-year-old being raised by a single father co-starring in a TV series in which he played a 5-year-old being raised by a single mother.

Marc's parents, both actors, separated when he was 6 months old. His father, John, assumed full custody. After a little more than a year, his mother moved to Europe, where she built a successful career. He never saw her again.

It was John's agent who thought of Marc for the role of Corey Baker, the son of a nurse being played by the accomplished Diahann Carroll. A real ground-breaker, Ms. Carroll, was the first black woman to star as a professional rather than a maid. The widow of a Vietnam vet, she struggled to balance work and home life with her son, Corey. The show was a hit. Diahann became the first black woman nominated for an Emmy for Best Actress in a comedy, and Marc Copage became one of television's first black child stars.

The two cast members grew close. "Ms. Carroll taught me to always be punctual and a person of my word, as she was. She came to the set on time for each show, completely prepared. She was polite to everyone and always careful about her diet. She would let me know if I started to get a little too pudgy. The producers would give me Bazooka bubble gum, but she would give me carob snacks that she thought were much healthier."

It went a bit beyond that for the motherless boy. He began asking if he could go home with her, and, for the first season, she said yes more than she said no. Marc loved it, but Diahann's daughter was understandably upset and the practice stopped. "I'm not quite sure at what point Ms. Carroll stopped being my mother in my mind."

After three years, *Julia* was canceled in 1971. The two stars kept in touch. Marc made a guest appearance on one of her television specials. He acted intermittently in *Cop Rock*, *Diff'rent Strokes*, *Sanford and Son*, and *The Kid*. He was deeply saddened to lose Diahann Carroll recently and remembered her lovingly in several written tributes.

Today, Marc works for a catering company. He is still very social with his former kid star friends of all ages. Among his many awards, he is included in the National Museum of African-American History and Culture and the Smithsonian, marking his great contribution to television history.

"As a kid, my favorite food was pizza—plain, just tomato sauce and cheese. As an adult, I must admit I still have a weakness for pizza, but now I like it with onions, mushrooms, jalapeños, turkey sausage, bell peppers, sometimes pineapple, pepperoni, sometimes garlic, sometimes pepperoncini, all depends on my mood. When I was younger, I had it several times a week. Those days are over. I am not much of a chef, but today, I try to eat a salad every day."

Marc's Simple Salad

Mixed greens
Fresh broccoli
sliced tomatoes
raisins

Toss with oil and vinegar and sprinkle with Feta cheese

Lassie: Timmy & Lassie

Jon Provost joined the original TV cast of Lassie in 1957 as a runaway found by the collie in the Miller barn. After half a season, Gramps dies, Ellen sells the farm, and Jeff leaves for college, but not before giving Lassie to young Timmy. Timmy stays on the farm with the new couple who buys it, Ruth and Paul Martin, played initially by Cloris Leachman and Jon Shepodd, replaced the following season by June Lockhart and Hugh Reilly. There Timmy would remain for seven years, syndicated in 120 countries. In 1964, when Provost left the show after 250 episodes, it was at its all-time high ranking.

Jon Provost

Jon Provost is beloved by millions for his portrayal of Timmy Martin on *Lassie*. The check shirt and jeans he wore hang in the Smithsonian next to Archie Bunker's chair; and he still receives letters and emails from fans of all ages around the world.

Jon was already a seasoned professional when he won the role of Timmy at age seven. It all began when Jon's mother read in Hedda Hopper's gossip column that Warner Bros. Studio was looking for a blonde, blue-eyed two to three-year-old boy to play Jane Wyman's son in a movie. Mrs. Provost loved Jane Wyman and thought she might be able to meet her and get her autograph. Ms. Wyman was not there, but 200 other little boys were… even little girls dressed to look like boys. At the end of a long day, Jon won the part and was signed by an agent present at the audition.

He was not quite 3 when he played the son of Jane Wyman and Sterling Hayden in *So Big*, and his mom got her autograph. More work followed with some of the biggest stars in Hollywood: Grace Kelly and Bing Crosby in *The Country Girl*, Rod Steiger and Anita Ekberg in *Back From Eternity*, William Holden and James Garner in *Towards the Unknown*, Clint Eastwood in *Escapade in Japan* and on television with Kim Novak, Joan Blondell, William Bendix and more. Jon was acclaimed as the top child actor of 1957.

Ron Howard anxiously awaits Jon's birthday cake

Then came *Lassie.* The boy and his dog embraced adventure in front of the cameras 5 days a week, 9 months a year. Jon also filmed commercials for the sponsor, Campbell's Soup, modeled clothes from the "Timmy and Lassie" line and made crossover appearances as Timmy on TV variety shows like *The Jack Benny Show* and *The Tennessee Ernie Ford Show.* On weekends and summers, he appeared with Lassie at rodeos, state fairs, and parades and solo at special events like the Indy 500. It left little time for friends and family. After 7 years, he'd had enough.

At 14, more interested in girls than dogs, Jon turned down offers to renew his contract and left the show in 1964.

He went to school, taking time off to work with TV's smartest horse, *Mr. Ed,* with Natalie Wood and Robert Redford in *This Property is Condemned, Secret of the Sacred Forest* with Gary Merrill in the Philippines and *The Computer Wore Tennis Shoes* with Kurt Russell. Now a teen heartthrob, he adorned the covers of *Tiger Beat* and *16 Magazine* along with TV appearances on *The Dating Game, The Dick Cavett Show* and *Happening '68* with Paul Revere and Mark Lindsay.

By the time Jon was 19, he'd worked in film and television for 16 years. With a strong desire to try something new, he headed for college in Northern California; and reveled in the first anonymity he'd ever known. The beauty of the wine country seduced him and Jon never returned to L.A., preferring eventually to raise a family in Sonoma County. Of his many accomplishments, he is most proud of his children, Ryan and Katie, and his grandchildren: Juliana, 5, and Lucas, not yet one.

Jon has also earned a nationwide reputation as a philanthropist, giving his time to children's hospitals, animal shelters and humane societies and, closest to his heart, Canine Companions for Independence, providing service dogs to the handicapped; and on whose Board of Governors he served for close to 25 years. He's received many awards, among them, The Motion Picture Council's Award for Outstanding Contribution as a Humanitarian for his dedication in helping the physically challenged, the Allen Ludden Humanitarian Award presented to him by Betty White and the Lifetime Achievement Award from the Youth in Film Association.

In 1990, Jon returned to television as Timmy all grown up in *The New Lassie* with Dee Wallace. He received a Genesis Award for Outstanding Television in a Family Series for a story he penned for the show focusing on the inhumane treatment of research animals. In1994, Jon was honored with a star on the Hollywood Walk of Fame.

In recent years, he added the internet to his resume, directing and hosting short videos about dogs and cats for a Purina website. 2008 marked Jon's 50th anniversary as Timmy. He celebrated with the release of his autobiography, *TIMMY'S IN THE WELL*.

Still a sought-after celebrity guest, Jon appears nationally at fund-raisers, comic cons, pet expos and special events throughout the year. Mischievous to the end, Jon says he still has some tricks up his sleeve. As they said at the end of many a Lassie episode, "To be continued!"

"This family recipe fills the house with wonderful aromas for hours as it cooks. That's the thing I remember as a kid—the second you entered the house you would smell that familiar smell and your mouth would water. I still love it. It's always a pleaser whether for two, a family or guests.

Jon Provost's Family Pot Roast

(Serves 4-6 people)

2-3 lb. chuck roast, boneless or 7 bone
1 med. white onion
4 big/med, 6 med/small potatoes
4 med. Carrots
Handful fresh green beans
Handful white mushrooms (optional, but I love them)
Center stalks of celery with the tender leaves
4-5 beef bouillon cubes
1 cup water
1/4 cup ketchup
1/3 cup red wine
a little olive oil
salt/pepper—up to you; but I think the dish makes all the taste you need.

Preheat your oven to 350 degrees. We're going to bake our pot roast for 2.5. hours.
Bring water to boil in small pan, add bouillon cubes and stir until dissolved.
Add ketchup and set aside.

Brown the roast in olive oil on both sides. Add onion (cut in eighths), pour bouillon mixture over all, cover and bake 1 hr.
I "swirl" my pan about every 20 min., but be careful when you swirl!
Add the red wine after the first swirl.

Hour 2: Add mushrooms (cut in 1/2 or 1/4 depending on size), carrots (cut 2.5/3 in long) and potatoes (halved depending on size).

Don't forget to swirl!
At the 45 min mark, add green beans (cut or not),
celery with greenery (cut 2 in) and bake about another 45 min.
You may want to adjust your cooking time depending on the
size of your vegetables or how firm you like them.
 Other than that it's a slam dunk. Enjoy!

"For years, Canine Companions had a celebrity chef competition as a fundraiser. I won
'Best Hot Hors d'oeuvre' several years running with this recipe. It sounds fancy, but it's easy
and people love it. It's fun to have a kid or a dog around to help, but not mandatory."

Jon's Curried Shrimp Puffs

(12 -15 servings)

1 cup bay shrimp
pinch of salt
1 egg white
fresh parsley
½ cup mayo
1 fresh baguette French bread
1-2 tsps yellow curry (to taste)

Beat egg white stiff.
Combine it with everything else except the parsley and bread.
Mix.
Slice bread, put dollop of mixture on bread. Broil till brown on top.
Sprinkle with fresh chopped parsley and serve immediately.

Lost in Space

Lost in Space chronicles the adventures of Professor John Robinson, Guy Williams, and his family: wife Maureen played by June Lockhart, two daughters, Judy and Penny played by Marta Kristen and Angela Cartwright and son Will portrayed by Bill Mumy. Traveling with them is U.S. Space Corps Major Donald West, Mark Goddard; and Jonathan Harris as the subversive stowaway, Dr. Zachary Smith, trapped on board.

These pioneers struggle to survive in the depths of space for 83 episodes over 3 seasons from September 15, 1965 to March 6, 1968.

Angela Cartwright

Artist, actress, author, photographer, curator, collaborator, instructor, traveler, wife, mother, and grandmother, not always in that order, Angela was born in Altrincham, Cheshire, England; and moved to Los Angeles, California with her family when she was 3 years old. She quickly began working as a child fashion model and appeared on numerous magazine covers and advertisements. She also made her film debut in *Somebody Up There Likes Me* as Paul Newman[1]s daughter. Another role followed in the movie *Something of Value* with Rock Hudson and Sidney Poitier.

At the age of 4, Danny Thomas signed Angela to play his daughter Linda Williams on the hit television series *Make Room for Daddy*, later called *The Danny Thomas Show*. The series ran for 7 years, during which time Angela starred in the Disney movie *Lad: A Dog*.

Following the Danny Thomas series, Angela was cast as Brigitta von Trapp in what would become one of the most popular films of all time, *The Sound of Music* starring Julie Andrews.In 1965, she was offered the role of Penny Robinson in the iconic series *Lost in Space*, which ran for 3 years. She has guest- starred in numerous television shows, commercials and movies.

Continuing to pursue her passion for art and photography, Angela authored *Mixed Emulsions – Altered Art Techniques for Photographic Imagery,* which explores her hand-

painted photography and her unique altered art techniques.

Two more art books followed, *In This House: A Collection of Altered Art Imagery and Collage Techniques*, and I*n This Garden: Explorations in Mixed Media Visual Narrative.* Angela also conceived and collaborated on *The Sound of Music Family Scrapbook* with her von Trapp siblings from the movie. (A revised version was released in 2020 celebrating the film's 55th anniversary.)

Angela continues to write articles on photo.art and altered art techniques and self publishes *Pasticcio Quartz* a Quality ART Zine. She has also pioneered and produced a clothing and jewelry line, Angela Cartwright Studio, which incorporates her hand- painted art.ography images on natural, easy to wear art and accessories.

Her art and photography, licensed for numerous products, is exhibited and collected around the world. Angela travels the world with Craftours teaching

her art techniques and annually leading a special trip to Salzburg, Austria sharing her *Sound of Music* behind the scenes experiences.

Angela's award-winning coffee table book *Styling the Stars: Lost Treasures from the Twentieth Century Fox Archive* offers an exclusive glimpse inside the studio's archives.

In celebration of the *Lost In Space* 50th Anniversary, Angela and her TV brother and life-long friend, Bill Mumy collaborated on a pictorial memoir, *Lost (and Found) In Space,* which offers never before seen photos and personal tales of their unique experiences while filming the show. They also spent several years collaborating on the recently published fantasy adventure novel *On Purpose.* The book includes original artwork by Angela; and Bill has written and produced a musical sound-track.

She married Steve in 1976, raised two children, Becca and Jesse, and is a grandmother of three.

"My fav dish as a child was Mom's baked custard. Whenever Veronica or I were sick, we asked her to make it. Being a Brit, that and a cuppa tea fixed anything that ailed you. Still does to this day."

Angela's Get Well Baked Custard

3 slightly beaten eggs
¼ cup sugar
2 cups milk, scalded
½ tsp vanilla
¼ tsp salt

Combine eggs, sugar and salt. Slowly stir in slightly cooled milk and vanilla.
Bake at 325 in a 1 quart casserole for 60 minutes or in six 5 oz. custard cups for 40-45 minutes.

I love to cook for my family. My stew is a staple around here when the weather turns chilly. Full of fresh vegetables it's hearty and healthy...

Angela's Boeuf Bourguignon (Beef Stew with Red Wine)

(Serves 6)

1 tablespoon good olive oil
8 ounces good bacon, diced
2-1/2 pounds beef chuck cut into 1inch cubes
Kosher salt
Freshly ground black pepper
1 pound carrots, sliced diagonally into 1 inch chunks
2 yellow onions, sliced
2 teaspoons chopped garlic (2 cloves)
1/2 cup Cognac or good brandy
1 (750-ml) bottle good dry red wine, such as Burgundy
2 to 2-1/2 cups canned beef broth
1 tablespoon tomato paste
1 teaspoon fresh thyme leaves
4 tablespoons (1/2 stick) unsalted butter, at room temperature, divided
3 tablespoons all purpose flour
1 pound frozen small whole onions
1 pound mushrooms, stems discarded, caps thickly sliced

For serving:

Country bread, toasted or grilled
1 garlic clove, cut in half
1/2 cup chopped fresh flat-leaf parsley (optional)

Preheat the oven to 250 degrees.
Heat the olive oil in a large Dutch oven, such as Le Creuset.
Add the bacon and cook over medium heat for 8 to 10 minutes, stirring occasionally, until the bacon is lightly browned.

Remove the bacon with a slotted spoon to a large plate. Dry the beef cubes with paper towels and then sprinkle them with salt and pepper. In batches in single layers, sear the beef in the hot oil for 3 to 5 minutes, turning to brown on all sides. Remove the seared cubes to the plate with the bacon and continue searing until all the beef is browned. Set aside.

Toss the carrots, onions, 1 tablespoon of salt, and 2 teaspoons of pepper (I might use less since I thought it was a bit too peppery) into the fat in the pan and cook over medium heat for 10 to 12 minutes, stirring occasionally, until the onions are lightly browned.

Add the garlic and cook for 1 more minute.
Add the Cognac, stand back, and ignite with a match to burn off the alcohol.
Put the meat and bacon back into the pot with any juices that have accumulated on the plate.

Add the wine plus enough beef broth to almost cover the meat.
Add the tomato paste and thyme.

Bring to a boil, cover the pot with a tight-fitting lid, and place it in the oven for about 1-1/4 hours, or until the meat and vegetables are very tender when pierced with a fork.

Remove from the oven and place on top of the stove.Combine 2 tablespoons of the butter and the flour with a fork and stir into the stew.
Add the frozen onions.

In a medium pan, sauté the mushrooms in the remaining 2 tablespoons of butter over medium heat for 10 minutes, or until lightly browned, and then add to the stew.

Bring the stew to a boil, then lower the heat and simmer uncovered for 15 minutes.
Season to taste.

Rub each slice of bread on one side with garlic.
For each serving, spoon the stew over a slice of bread and sprinkle with parsley.
If the sauce is too thin, you can add more of the butter and flour mixture.

To make in advance, cook the stew and refrigerate. To serve, reheat to a simmer over low heat and serve with the bread and parsley. (It's actually more flavorful made a day ahead!)"

Bill Mumy

Bill Mumy is a multi-talented, prolific artist who entered show business at the age of five. He has worked in over 400 television shows; and is best known by his many fans around the world for his memorable roles as the heroic boy astronaut, Will Robinson in the classic series *Lost in Space*, Anthony Fremont from *The Twilight Zone* and Lennier from the popular science fiction series *Babylon 5* in which he co-starred for 5 years. Currently, Bill is a consulting producer on the long-running television series, *Ancient Aliens*.

A member of the Academy of Motion Picture Arts and Sciences, Bill has also been in 18 feature films, including *Dear Brigitte, Rascal, Bless the Beasts and Children*, and *Papillion*.

A voice-over artist, Bill has narrated over 50 episodes of A&E's *Biography* as well as hosting and narrating several documentaries and specials for A&E, The SyFy Channel and E! Entertainment. In 2015, he gave voice to President Abraham Lincoln for The History Channel's *Civil War: Blood and Glory* miniseries. His voice can also be heard on animated shows like *Rescue Bots, Bravest Warriors, Ren and Stimpy, Scooby Doo, Batman: The Animated Series*, Steven Spielberg's *Animaniacs, Little Wizard Adventures, The Oz Kids* and Disney's *Buzz Lightyear: Star Command* as well as dozens of national commercials.

2015 marked the 50th anniversary of *Lost in Space* with an impressive 18-disc BluRay release. The bonus material features an original cast performance of Bill's script, *The Epilogue,* which resolves the classic series. Bill co-produced, directed, wrote and starred in the bonus material which won a Gold Clio Award in 2016 for Best Creative Content. To coincide with the golden anniversary, Bill has co-written a book with his *Lost in Space* "sister", Angela Cartwright, *Lost (and Found) in Space* featuring photographs and memories of filming the classic series. Bill also collaborated with Angela on the recently published fantasy novel *On Purpose* and wrote and produced a soundtrack for the book.

With acclaimed writer Peter David, Bill co-created, produced and wrote *Space Cases,* a live action sci-fi adventure comedy series on Nickelodeon syndicated in over 60 countries. The series ran for 2 seasons, 1996-97; and was nominated for a Cable Ace Award for Best Children's Series. He also co-wrote its theme song as well as the themes for the 2003 Animal Planet specials: *50 Greatest Animals of TV* and *50 Greatest Animals of Films* as well as *TV Guide Looks At...*, *Hollywood Backstory*, and *Studio Portraits*. He's written dozens of songs and themes to many different film and television projects; and was nominated for an Emmy for Outstanding Achievement in Music Direction and Composition for the live-action Disney series *Adventures in Wonderland*. He wrote and recorded an amazing 105 songs for the 100 episodes of that series.

Bill is half of the infamous novelty rock recording and short film-making duo Barnes and Barnes. Best known for the classic demented song and film *Fish Heads,* Barnes and Barnes have released nine albums and a feature length video. *Rolling Stone Magazine* named *Fish Heads* #57 of the all-time greatest rock videos ever created.

Bill is a prolific songwriter and solo recording artist with many solo CD's and solo music videos, among them: *Velour, Ten Days, Illuminations, Until The Big Bang Whimpers, Glorious in Defeat, Carnival Sky, Speechless, Circular, The Landlord Or The Guest, With Big Ideas, Ghosts, After Dreams Come True, Pandora's Box, In The Current,* and *Dying To Be Heard.* He has worked with the pop group America off and on for over 30 years, composing, producing and performing with the band.

His most current musical project is the release of *Angels Hear,* the debut album of a new rock group, ACTION SKULLS, featuring Bill, Vicki Peterson of The Bangles and John Cowsill of The Beach Boys and The Cowsills.

Comic books have been a passion since childhood and Bill has written scores of them for both Marvel and DC. He also wrote the *Lost in Space* comic book for Innovation and the acclaimed 360-page graphic novel, *Lost in Space: Voyage to the Bottom of the Soul.* 2013 saw the release of his *Curse of the Mumy comic book* for Bluewater comics. His short stories, *The Black '59* and *The Undeadliest Game,* co-written with Peter David, printed in *Shock Rock* and *Shock Rock Volume 2* have been translated into many languages.

Bill lives with his wife Eileen and their many dogs in Laurel Canyon. Their two children, Seth and Liliana, have also made their mark as actors. When *TV Guide* listed their top 100 television episodes of all time, 2 of them starred Bill Mumy.

"Hard to believe we ever actually ate this... I haven't eaten any red meat in 40 years... BUT... when I was a kid, my dad and I made these sandwiches all the time and we loved 'em.

The Mumy Super Dooper Sandwich

2 pieces white Wonder bread
Spread a generous helping of Skippy creamy peanut butter on one piece of bread
Add 1 slice Kraft American cheese
Add some thinly sliced roast beef or a piece of Oscar Meyer bologna
(!!) (No, I'm not kidding.)
Add 1 piece of very cold Iceberg lettuce...eat!

As for a modern Mumy recipe... This is a standard around Mumy Manor...

Mumy's Laurel Canyon Vegetable Soup

We eyeball our portions depending on the size of the pot we use or how many people are here... so good luck. You can't really screw this up. All ingredients are best if organic and from local farmers.

Add some corn
Add some Broccoli
Add some garbanzo beans
Add some red kidney beans
Add half a bunch chopped cilantro
Chop carrots into very small pieces
Chop and add some potato pieces
Chop and add some green beans
Chop and add some onion
Chop and add some celery

Cut and add some mushroom pieces
Chop some tomatoes in a blender
Sauté all the ingredients in fresh minced garlic and olive oil
When the veggies are translucent, add a box of vegetable broth and a small can of tomato sauce
Season with a little Lawry's garlic salt
Season with some Cholula hot sauce
Add fresh jalapeno or chili flakes (depending on how spicy you want it)
Simmer for 45 minutes
Serve with melted shredded mozzarella or provolone cheese on top (Yes, it'll stick to your spoon)
Warm up a heel of fresh French Bread...eat!"

Margie

Margie starred Cynthia Pepper as a teenage girl growing up in a small New England town during the Roaring Twenties. The series was adapted from a 1946 film which starred Jeanne Crain. It ran one season (26 episodes) on ABC from October 12, 1961 to April 12, 1962.

Cynthia Pepper

Cynthia Anne Culpepper was born in Hollywood, California; and was drawn early to an acting career by her parents, vaudeville and night club entertainer Jack Pepper and his second wife Dawn (Stanton) Pepper, a former dancer who once worked for showman Billy Rose. Her father was previously married and divorced from Ginger Rogers.

Cynthia started out in New York, at the tender age of 3, as a Conover child model. A year or so later, she briefly appeared on Broadway in a tiny part in *It's a Gift*, starring Julie Harris. Outside of an unbilled part, at age 10, in the movie, *Cheaper by the Dozen*, Cynthia did not actively pursue acting until returning to Los Angeles and graduating from Hollywood High School. A year later, at 19, she married Buck Edwards, who was also in the business behind the scenes.

Once she found an agent, the work offers came. One of her first sightings was as a "malt shop girl" in the comedy series, *The Many Loves of Dobie Gillis*, starring Dwayne Hickman. Following that, she found work on two popular ABC detective series: *Bourbon Street Beat* with Richard Long and *77 Sunset Strip* with Efrem Zimbalist Jr., Roger Smith, and Edd "Kookie" Byrnes.

Cynthia's career gained momentum, when she won a regular role in the all-male *My Three Sons* sitcom as the girlfriend of the oldest son, Mike, played by Tim Considine. On the strength of her popularity in that role, she was offered her own series, *Margie* as "Roaring 20s" teen flapper Margie Clayton. It lasted just one season, but 20th Century-Fox planned to build another series around her. However, the financial debacle of Elizabeth Taylor's *Cleopatra* bankrupted the studio, and they were forced to let her go.

Undaunted, Cynthia found work in films. She starred opposite Sandra Dee in *Take Her, She's Mine* before winning the co-starring role of PFC Midge Riley, opposite the one and only Elvis Presley, in *Kissin' Cousins*. Later that year, she returned to *My Three Sons* to film one final appearance as Considine's now- former girlfriend, who learns that Mike has become engaged to another woman.

Assorted TV guest parts followed, including *Perry Mason*, *The Addams Family*, *Julia*, *Family*, and *The Flying Nun*.

Cynthia married in 1959 and gave birth to a son, Michael, in 1965. Three years later, she divorced. She married James Pazillo in 1969 and chose to leave show business to focus on her marriage and raising her son.

These days, Cynthia can be spotted at Elvis gatherings around the world or signing autographs at nostalgic conventions. She made a rare appearance in the film, *Miss Congeniality 2: Armed and Fabulous,* starring Sandra Bullock in 2005.

"Coffee Dan's on Highland and Hollywood Boulevard was my favorite place. I used to walk from Hollywood High after school for fries and cherry-coke with a group or with my best friend. Before we left, we'd always sign the napkins. She'd write 'Grace Kelly was here' and I'd put 'Debbie Reynolds was here.' We left it every time."

Cindy's Cherry Coke

3/4 cup Coca-Cola
1 tablespoon grenadine syrup
1 tablespoon maraschino cherry juice

Stir together the cola, grenadine, and cherry juice.
Pour over ice with a cherry on top and serve immediately.

"As an adult, my favorite dinner of all time is steak and rice served with cooked spinach and followed by pecan pie topped with whipped cream.
LOVE it.

Cynthia's Spinach

Wash an entire bag of spinach in salt water which kills any bacteria and bugs.
Rinse and drain.
Throw it in a pot with a little olive oil, onion, and tiny pieces of garlic.
Let it cook down.

That's it! Easy and delicious!"

The Monroes

The Monroes follows the trials of five orphans fighting to survive on the frontier after their parents die in an accident. Michael Anderson and Barbara Hershey played the oldest siblings, Clay and Kathy. Keith and Kevin Schultz were twins Jefferson and Fennimore while Tammy Locke rounded out the cast as the youngest Monroe, Amy. It aired on ABC for one season in '66-'67 for 26 episodes.

Keith and Kevin Schultz

Keith and Kevin Schultz are twins who were just infants when they made their screen debut in the film *The Long Gray Line.*

"It was an accident that I got the twins into the business," said their late mom, Evelyn. "The girl across the street told Central Casting about them. They immediately worked and just kept going from job to job, just by word of mouth. Then somebody said, 'Who is their agent?' and I told my husband, 'I guess I'm supposed to have an agent.'"

They got that agent. And commercials, movies, and TV work kept coming. Then in 1966, at age 13, Keith and Kevin landed co-starring roles in the television series *The Monroes*, portraying pioneering twin brothers Jefferson "Big Twin" Monroe and Fennimore "Little Twin" Monroe respectively. Though only one season, *The Monroes* launched the brothers as child stars and 'tween idols which kept the pair busy on talk shows, teen magazine covers, and personal appearances across the country.

Next, Kevin won the role of Tom Sawyer in the Hanna-Barbera television series *The New Adventures of Huckleberry Finn*, the first weekly television series to combine live-action performers with animation. The show continued in reruns for some 40+ years! With their success as teen idols established, the natural move in 1967 was to form a rock band. The Monroe Doctrine was born with Greg Reinhardt and older brother Ric Schultz.

In 1970, known as Keith, Kevin & Air, the group signed a record deal and released a single with their most memorable songs, *Euphoria* and *Michael's Theme*.

Offers to act continued. Keith guest-starred on *Gunsmoke*, *The Flying Nun* and *Cannon*. Kevin guested on: *The Iron Horse*, *Lucas Tanner* and *Eight is Enough*, as well as appearing in the celebrated surfer film *Big Wednesday* with Jan-Michael Vincent and Gary Busey.

Her sons' fame changed Evelyn's life too. "Over the years, I sent her (the agent) people… and she thought I had a good eye for talent. I went to work for her. She retired and I took over, and I was one of the top children's agents for 30 years. Look what unfolded."

What would end up as the twins' final appearance came in 1986 and would fittingly be together as brothers Ken and K.C. Zeigler on the ground-breaking Showtime comedy series

Brothers. At that point, Keith and Kevin, young men by then, looked to do something more fulfilling.

The guys shared a passion for photography while working in front of the cameras, so it was a fairly smooth transition for them to work together behind the camera shooting celebrities. Keith is the photographer while Kevin handles the lighting and any retouching or restoration. The brothers have worked almost as long as photographers as they did as actors. And it should be no mystery that they are best known for their head shots of child stars like Mary-Kate and Ashley Olsen, Jonathan Taylor Thomas and Raven-Symoné, among others.

"As kids, we liked frog legs! We would get them only in the Southern states like North and South Carolina and Florida and Georgia when we were doing personal appearances…fried, of course! And we both loved Mom's cheese pie."

Evelyn Schultz's Cheese Pie

(10-12 servings, cut thinly, VERY rich.)

2 cups graham cracker crumbs
Mix with ½ cup sugar and ½ cup melted butter.
 Press into the bottom and up the sides of a 9" spring-form pan to form a crust.
Cream 2 8 oz packages of cream cheese, softened, until smooth.
Blend in 2 eggs, 2/3 c. sugar and 1 tsp. vanilla.
Pour into crust and bake in 375 degree oven for 20 minutes.
Remove from oven and let pie stand 15 minutes.
Meanwhile, combine 1 c. commercial sour cream with 2 Tbs. sugar and 1 tsp. vanilla.
Carefully spread over baked filling.
Return pie to a very hot oven (425 deg.) and bake for 10 minutes.
 Cool pie, then chill overnight before serving before serving.

As adults, the guys still make this dish their mom taught them. "Best Mom ever. The older we get, the more we appreciate her. We still can't figure out how she had time to cook."

Evelyn's Every-day Meatloaf

(Serves 8)

2/3 cup dry bread crumbs
1 cup milk
1 ½ lbs. ground beef
2 slightly beaten eggs
¼ cup grated onion
1 tsp. salt
1/8 tsp. pepper
½ tsp. sage

Piquant Sauce: Combine
    3 tbs. brown sugar,
    ¼ c. catsup,
    ¼ tsp. nutmeg and
    1 tsp. dry mustard

Soak bread crumbs in milk;
 add meat eggs, onion and seasonings; mix well.
Form in individual loaves and place in greased muffin pans.
Cover meat loaves with Piquant Sauce.
 Bake in moderate oven (350 deg.) 45 minutes;
Or form in a single loaf in 4 ¾ x 8 ¾-inch loaf pan.
Spread sauce over it and bake 1 hour.

The Munsters

The Munsters, just like the Cleavers and the Andersons, were a typical American family except for the fact they were monsters. Papa Herman, a Frankenstein type, was played by Fred Gwynne. Yvonne De Carlo portrayed his vampire wife, Lily. Al Lewis, another vampire, embodied 378-year-old Gramps. Beverley Owen (later replaced by Pat Priest) was their unfortunate niece, Marilyn, whose normal, all-American looks made the rest of the family feel sorry for her; and Butch Patrick as their werewolf son, Eddie. *The Munsters,* who lived at 1313 Mockingbird Lane in the fictional California suburb of Mockingbird Heights, could never quite figure out why the neighbors had such a strange reaction to them. The series aired on Thursday at 7:30 pm on CBS from September 24, 1964, to May 12, 1966, for 70 episodes.

Butch Patrick

In 1960, seven-year-old Patrick Lilley went on a photoshoot with his little sister. She was the subject, but it was "Butch's" headshot that would wind up in the studio's Hollywood Boulevard window. Utilizing his nickname and real first name, his agent and his mom, Patti, created the stage name, Butch Patrick. Butch met with almost instant success, landing his first three auditions: a movie starring Eddie Albert and Jane Wyatt, called *The Two Little Bears*; a soap opera, *General Hospital* in their first year; and an award-winning Kellogg's Corn Flakes commercial. Butch continued to work consistently throughout the early '60s on the most popular TV programs of the time like *Mister Ed, My Favorite Martian, The Untouchables, Ben Casey, Rawhide, Gunsmoke, Bonanza* and many more.

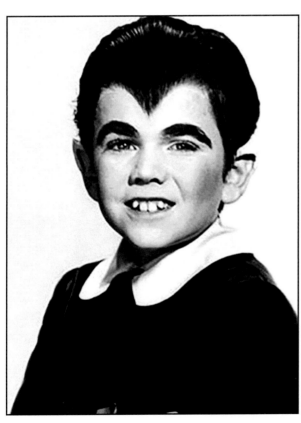

A second series came his way with the reboot of the classic *The Real McCoys*. Working with Oscar winner Walter Brennan and Richard Crenna was a huge treat for Butch. During the series, he also worked in over 20 commercials and a dozen movies with stars like Burt Lancaster, Judy Garland, Mickey Rooney, Jo Van Fleet, Sal Mineo, Don Murray, Edward G. Robinson, to name just a few.

In 1964, Butch got a call to report to CBS Studio Center for a screen test. It was a call that changed his life. His screen test was with the famous movie star Yvonne De Carlo, and his character was Edward Wolfgang Munster. From that day on, Butch would be known worldwide as the iconic Eddie Munster. Fifty years later, *The Munsters* is still one of the most popular series of the 1960s. Certainly no one had a more recognizable hairline.

After a two-year stint, Butch made two films for Disney's *Wonderful World of Color,* shot several features, and appeared on 10 episodes of *My Three Sons* as well as appearances on *Adam 12*, the pilot episode of *Marcus Welby, M.D.*, *Ironside* and more. Then, in 1971, Sid Krofft took Butch to lunch and convinced him to star in their new show for Sid and Marty's World *Lidsville*.

After Butch turned 19, he chose to leave Hollywood. He formed a band, Eddie and the Monsters, drove fast cars, and spent time surfing. During this time, he indulged in drug and alcohol use which led to a decades-long battle for sobriety. After 40 years, he is proud to say he has been drug and alcohol free since 2010.

Today, Butch works the indie movie circuit, giving back to the industry that served him well. He's a cancer survivor and works with people with addiction issues. He has also launched a new YouTube channel where he highlights interesting stories from America.

"My favorite thing to eat as a kid was tacos. Typically, we weren't allowed to watch TV when we ate dinner. But the whole family loved a new show called *The Flintstones*. Once a week, we would set up the TV trays in the family room. Mom would make tacos and we'd watch *The Flintstones*. Dad always rushed home for it. He'd just gotten a new 1960 Cadillac. It was so long, it barely fit in the garage. It was time for dinner when Dad's bumper hit the wall in the garage. The room would shake and the TV tables would wobble...every Wednesday night. Yabba Dabba Doo!"

Butch's Favorite Tacos

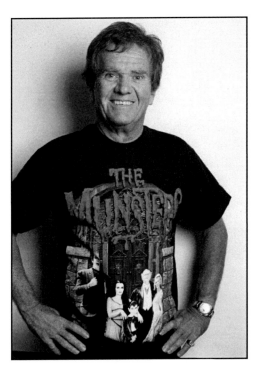

1lb. lean ground beef
1 medium onion, chopped
1 teaspoon chili powder
½ teaspoon salt
½ teaspoon garlic powder
1 (8-oz.) can tomato sauce
12 taco shells
6oz. (1 1/2 cups) shredded American
or Cheddar cheese
2 cups shredded lettuce
2 tomatoes, chopped
¾ cup salsa
¾ cup sour cream, if desired

Heat oven to 250°F.
In medium skillet, brown ground beef and onion over medium heat for 8 to 10 minutes or until beef is thoroughly cooked, stirring frequently. Drain.
Stir in chili powder, salt, garlic powder and tomato sauce.
Reduce heat to low; cover and simmer 10 minutes.
Meanwhile, place taco shells on ungreased cookie sheet.
Heat at 250°F. for 5 minutes.
To assemble tacos, layer beef mixture, cheese, lettuce and tomatoes in each taco shell.
Serve with salsa. Top with sour cream.

My Three Sons

l to r: Fred MacMurray, Beverly Garland, Don Grady, Tina Cole, Stan and Barry Livingston, William Demarest, Dawn Lyn, and Tramp

My Three Sons starred Fed MacMurray as widower and aeronautical engineer, Steven Douglas who is raising his three sons: Mike, Robbie and Chip played by Tim Considine, Don Grady and Stanley Livingston. In later years, Steve Douglas remarries and adopts his new wife's young daughter, Dodie, played by Dawn Lyn. He has help from his late wife's father, Bub, played by William Frawley who lives with them as cook and housekeeper. Frawley retired in 1965 due to illness and was replaced by William Demarest, playing Bub's brother, Uncle Charley.

In September 1965, eldest son Mike marries and is written out of the show. Enter Chip's orphan friend Ernie, played by Stan Livingston's real-life brother, Barry, who is adopted as the "new" third son. The series had a 12-year run, from 1960 through 1972 with 380 episodes, making it the third longest-running sitcom in TV history.

Stanley Livingston

Stanley Livingston can already boast sixty years in the entertainment industry—including a phenomenal twelve-year run as Chip Douglas on one of television's most popular and durable series, *My Three Sons*. The Emmy-nominated and Golden Globe-winning series has been broadcast continuously for over 55 years.

Stan's career began at the tender age of four when he performed with an underwater swim group called the WATER BABIES. TV appearances and magazine articles brought him to the attention of agents, and, at five, Stan turned actor appearing as a neighborhood kid on *The Adventures of Ozzie and Harriet*. Stan was a semi-regular for four seasons, until 1960, when he began his role of Chip on *My Three Sons*.

Stanley also appeared on the big screen in ten feature films including *Rally 'Round the Flag, Boys* with Paul Newman and Joanne Woodward; *The Bonnie Parker Story* with Dorothy Provine; *Please Don't Eat the Daisies* with Doris Day and David Niven; *X-15* with Charles Bronson and Mary Tyler Moore; *How the West Was Won* (the last Cinerama movie ever made) with Debbie Reynolds and George Peppard; *Private Parts* (the Paul Bartel cult classic); *Hotwire* with James Keach and *Attack of the 60 Foot Centerfold*.

Following its primetime run, *My Three Sons* immediately went into syndication, airing daily for the next thirteen years. In 1985, Nickelodeon began airing the vintage black and white episodes several times a day; and the series became a smash hit with a whole new generation. The show also helped launch the TV LAND Network in 1995, and is still seen both in the US and in amany countries around the world.

At his many appearances, Stan was regularly asked for advice on how to get into show business. It led to a decade-long project interviewing hundreds of directors, casting agents, actors, and more to create the quintessential response.

THE ACTOR'S JOURNEY is an Eight Volume (ten-hour long) DVD Program that focused entirely on the Business (or non-performance) Aspects of an actor's career. "The Actor's Journey" is for adult actors and performers (18 years of age and older).

THE ACTOR'S JOURNEY for KIDS is a Five Volume (five-hour long) DVD Program that teaches the parents of child and teen actors and performers everything about the Business Aspects of their child or teen's career. "The Actor's Journey for Kids" is for the parents of child and teen actors (through 17 years of age).

These DVD programs are the quintessential education programs on the business and career development aspects of an acting career, a "must-see" for anyone considering, or actively pursuing a career as an actor or performer in today's highly competitive entertainment industry.

Stan is the owner of First Team Productions. Over the years, the production company has produced feature films, television pilots, episodic television segments, documentaries, commercials, PBS-style programming, music and educational videos, shorts and even a 3-Strip 35mm CINERAMA® Process Film. And Stan has worked in a multitude of positions, including director, producer, executive producer, writer, editor, cinematographer and, of course, as an actor.

"We had seven people in our family. I always had two or three friends hanging around the house at dinner time. Bless her heart, Mom created this dish. It was easy for her to make, tasty and cheap —and everybody's favorite. My Dad continued the tradition after my mom died in '79. If you make the hamburger and rice dish just once, you will be hooked for life! I know Barry and I are!

Stan and Barry's Favorite Childhood Recipe

(serves 3)

1 lb of hamburger
1 stick of butter
2 cans of Campbell's cream of mushroom soup
White rice
1 can of sliced pineapple

Melt ½ stick of butter in a large, deep iron skillet.
Add 1 pound of hamburger meat and brown.
After meat is brown on the outside, break into small chunks.
Continue to stir meat until raw, pink color inside disappears.
Add 2 cans of cream of mushroom soup.
Continue to simmer and stir.

While meat is cooking, make 1 cup of white rice.
When mushroom soup starts to bubble, it's ready to serve (about 10 minutes)

Serve hamburger and mushroom soup over a bed of white rice with pineapple slices on the side.

As for my favorite recipe today, I make a great guacamole that's requested at every party my wife, Paula, and I throw.

Stan's Famous Guacamole

3 avocados
2 tomatoes
1 onion
1 bunch of cilantro
1 lime
1 small can diced mild chili peppers

Peel and cut avocados in half and remove pits. chop all ingredients.
Divide chopped ingredients into 3 sections with one whole avocado per group
Add one group of ingredients into blender and blend on low speed, turning blender on and off.
When off, push ingredients to the bottom with a wooden spoon
Repeat with 2nd and 3rd groups until all 3 groups have been blended together

On 3rd group, add salt, pepper and garlic to taste. Blend all 3 groups together.

Notes:
The less you blend, the chunkier it will be. The more you blend, the creamier it will be.

Put an avocado pit at the bottom of the serving bowl. It will keep the guacamole from turning dark.
Serve the guacamole with Doritos nacho flavored chips"

Barry Livingston

Barry Livingston was just 4 when he was cast as Paul Newman's son in the film, *Rally Round the Flag Boys*. Sadly, he was abruptly fired when his eyes developed astigmatism, requiring him to wear glasses. As luck would have it, his horn-rimmed spectacles became his trademark and established him as a new type of child actor: a prototype nerd with glasses, buckteeth, and unruly hair.

After a recurring role on *The Adventures of Ozzie & Harriet*, Barry found national fame when cast as Ernie Douglas on the classic TV series *My Three Sons*, which ran for a phenomenal twelve years.

After *Sons*, Barry went to New York to be in the Broadway production of *The Skin of Our Teeth*, directed by Jose Quintero.

Other stage roles followed in *Cause Celebre* at the Ahmanson Theatre in Los Angeles, Bertesgaden off-Broadway, *The Third DayComes* directed by John Cassavetes, and the musical *You're A Good Man, Charlie Brown*. After establishing himself on stage, Barry returned to TV appearing in such classics as *Room 222*, *The Streets of San Francisco* and *Ironsides* in the '70s; *Simon & Simon*, *Hart to Hart* and *Doogie Howser, M.D.* in the '80s; and *The Nanny*, *Ally McBeal* and *Lois & Clark: The New Adventures of Superman* in the '90s.

In the new millennium, Barry has appeared in *The Orville, NCIS: Los Angeles,* *The Fosters, Castle, NCIS, Major Crimes, Mistresses, Grey's Anatomy, Hot in Cleveland, Two and a Half Men, Big Love* and *Mad Men*. He's also been busy on the big screen in *Dickie Roberts, First Daughter, Zodiac, Horrible Bosses, You Don't Mess With The Zohan, Jersey Boys, The Social Network, Argo* and *War Dogs*.

As Barry enters his 63rd year in the industry, he's lost the buck teeth and the unruly hair, but the work keeps on coming.

"For my fave recipe as an adult, I admit I'm not much of a cook myself, but my wife, Karen, makes a mean turkey and this scalloped corn dish that I love.

Barry's Favorite Scalloped Corn Dish

2 eggs
1 can creamed corn
1 can regular corn
½ stick of butter – melted
1 small onion
1 cup sour cream
½ pound of cheddar cheese
¾ cup cornbread mix

Blend all ingredients using only ½ the cheese. Bake at 375° for 35 minutes. Sprinkle with remaining cheese. Bake another 10 minutes. Serve immediately and be prepared for compliments!

Words are not enough for this beautiful dish. You have to see it…then you have to taste it. Delicious!"

Dawn Lyn

Dawn Lyn made her acting debut at the tender age of 4, playing a Native American in a low budget Western. It wasn't until she was 12 that she found out she was credited as having played a boy!

At 5, she was cast as Prudence in the pilot for *Nanny and the Professor*. When the show did not sell right away, the producers released her from her contract. Immediately, Dawn was scooped up for the role of Dodie in *My Three Sons*, her most fondly remembered work. At the last minute, *Nanny* sold. The producers sued *My Three Sons* trying to regain their star, but there was nothing to be done. She remained in the role of Dodie for three years until the show came to an end in 1972.

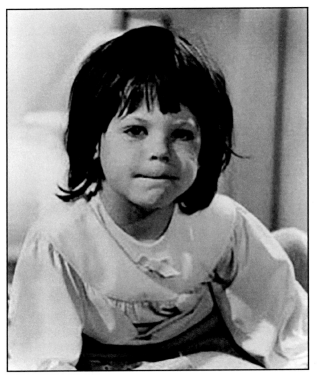

In 1971 Dawn landed a major role in the Western, *Shoot-Out* as the daughter of screen legend Gregory Peck. Mr. Peck proved a real-life hero on the set when he caught Dawn as she fell while attempting a dangerous stunt, and saved her from serious injury.

Dawn worked steadily throughout the 1970s in shows like *The Bold Ones, Gunsmoke, Mannix, Marcus Welby, M.D., Adam-12, Harry O, Barnaby Jones* and *The Streets of San Francisco*. She supported her mother and brother, Leif Garrett who was beginning an acting career of his own. They played on-screen sister and brother in the *Walking Tall* film trilogy, and again in an episode of *Cannon*. She won a recurring role as

Reagan in the popular series *Born Free*. She also had a recurring role in the 1977 series *The Red Hand Gang*. Her last onscreen appearance was in a 1978 episode of *Wonder Woman* which starred her brother as a character similar to himself—a teen pop star—while Dawn played his devoted fan.

As her brother's career took off, Dawn's began to slow. Her petite stature of 4' 10 began to work against her as she aged. She decided to branch out professionally, teaching acting

and working as an in-demand spokesperson. While living in Avalon on Catalina Island from 1997 to 2006, Dawn performed with the Avalon Community Theater Radio Troupe. Today, she and her husband live in Hawaii.

"When I was a kid, we loved going to Solvang because it was a reasonable distance to drive, and it is very charming. I am half Scandinavian, mostly Norwegian and a bit Danish, so we loved that it is basically a model of a Danish town. We visited 2 or 3 times a year. We always stayed at Svengaards when we were there. They had an old fashioned telephone system, the kind with the red and black cords you had to plug into certain places to connect an incoming call to a room. They showed me how to operate it and let me answer the phones for a while. I was about 9 years old and I had so much fun. We would go to the restaurant that served only waffles with various toppings…not sure if it's still there…whipped cream covering the waffle and everything but the kitchen sink on top: bananas, strawberries, walnuts, peaches, blueberry jam, powdered sugar…amazing!

I acquired the following recipe many years ago as a photocopied handout from a small town 'mom and pop store.' These carrot cakes proved to be quite popular with my family when I gave them as Christmas presents. I have 2 cousins, brothers Peter and Steven, who, year after year, hide their own cake trying to con each other into sharing theirs. It never works. They each go home with their own whole meatloaf-sized cake.

In the past, the most tedious and time-consuming part was grating the carrots. Now I just get bags of pre-grated carrots.

Dawn's Favorite Carrot Cake

In a large bowl:
       3 eggs well beaten
       1.5 cups sugar
       2.5 tsp. hot water
       1 cup oil
       2 cups grated carrots
       1.5 cups flour
       1 tsp. baking powder
       .25 tsp. salt
       .50 tsp. nutmeg
       .50 tsp. cinnamon

Mix ingredients well.
Add 1 cup chopped walnuts (optional).
In an ungreased pan, bake at 350 degrees for 1 hour.
Cream cheese frosting is also optional."

The Patty Duke Show

The Patty Duke Show revolves around the lives of two sixteen-year-old identical cousins. Patty Lane is a normal, high-spirited teenager living in Brooklyn Heights, New York. Cathy is a shy, European sophisticate.

Patty's father, Martin (William Schallert), is the managing editor of the New York Daily Chronicle; Cathy's father, Kenneth (also played by Schallert), is Martin's identical twin brother and a foreign correspondent for the same paper. Cathy moves to the United States from Scotland to live with Patty's family until her father returns home. The girls are identical physically and can imitate each other's voice, but are near polar opposites in lifestyle and taste. That's where the comedy comes in. Jean Byron played Natalie, Patty's mother, Paul O'Keefe was Ross, her brother and Eddie Applegate played Patty's boyfriend, Richard. The show ran on ABC from September 18, 1963 to April 27, 1966 with 105 episodes.

Patty Duke

Patty Duke was sensational. In 1963 when *The Patty Duke Show* premiered, her amazing energy and abundant talent combined to create BOTH sides of the perfect teenage girl. She embodied the quintessential American teen, Patty Lane, and then, with the flip of a curl and the twist of a headband, she became her identical twin cousin, Cathy Lane, a more proper, worldly Scottish girl. The popular comedy attracted big stars like Rat Packers Sammy Davis, Jr. and Peter Lawford and teen heartthrob Sal Mineo. It earned Patty an Emmy nomination and also launched a recording career for her.

Born in New York City, Patty started her career in print ads, commercials, and soap opera work. Her big break came October 1959 when she opened on Broadway in *The Miracle Worker* playing the blind, deaf-mute, Helen Keller, opposite the brilliant Anne Bancroft as her teacher, Annie Sullivan. The women pulled in standing-room crowds until July 1961. Then it was Hollywood's turn. The 1962 film starring Patty and Ms. Bancroft earned both actresses Oscars: Best Actress for Bancroft and Best Supporting Actress for 16-year-old Patty who, at that time, was the youngest person to receive an Academy Award in a competitive category.

After the cancellation of *The Patty Duke Show* in 1966, Patty famously played Neely O'Hara in *Valley of the Dolls*. In 1969, she won a Golden Globe for Best Actress in *Me, Natalie*. In all, Patty had 10 Emmy nominations with three wins, all in the '70s. The first for a made-for-TV movie, *My Sweet Charlie,* the second for the TV miniseries *Captains and the Kings* and her third win for the 1979 TV movie *The Miracle Worker*, this time playing Anne Sullivan to Melissa Gilbert's Helen Keller. She also garnered 4 nominations for Golden Globes with 2 wins.

A gifted actress, well-respected by her peers, in 1985, Patty became the second woman elected president of the Screen Actors Guild, a post she held until 1988.

Though Patty knew the dizzying heights of fame, she also experienced tremendous lows. Few people knew of her emotional struggles until 1987 when she revealed in her autobiography the terrible abuse she suffered as a child left in the care of her cruel and unscrupulous managers. She also disclosed that for decades, she'd suffered with mental illness, manic depression (known now as bipolar disorder). One of the first public figures to bravely speak out, Patty led the way as an activist for mental health causes.

Patty took occasional TV roles in the 2000s with her final appearance, guest-starring on *Liv and Maddie* fittingly as a pair of identical twins. A few months later, to the shock and sadness of her family, friends and many fans, Patty Duke died on March 29, 2016, from sepsis caused by "a ruptured intestine." She was 69.

Her website posted this message:
An amazing life force who helped so many with her sensitive work and her generous public revelations on mental health. A true survivor, Patty Duke left a remarkable legacy.
The world is a better place because she was in it.

Cousin Cathy loved "the minuet, the Ballet Russe and crepe Suzettes…"

Cathy Lane's Crepe Suzettes with Orange Sauce

(12 pancakes/serves 6)

2 cups plain flour
½ tsp salt
6 eggs
2 cups milk

Sift flour and salt together in a bowl.
In another bowl, beat the six eggs together until they are "lemony" looking.
Then beat in 2 cups of milk. Pour the liquid into the flour and mix quickly until blended.
 As soon as the flour disappears, that's enough!
Heat a 5-inch frying pan and coat it with butter. Take the frying pan off the heat.
Here comes the tricky part. Pour in a tblsp of batter and dip the pan back and forth so
 the batter smoothes out to the edges of the pan. Set the pan back on the heat for a couple
of minutes.
When the pancake is a light golden brown on one side, turn it over. This is best done with
 the fingers or a spatula. The other side cooks more quickly, in no more than half a minute.
Keep in a warm oven on a pie pan until they're all made.
Next, roll them up, arrange on a plate and pour the orange sauce over

Orange Sauce

1/3 cup orange juice
3 tblsps lemon juice
Grated rind of ½ an orange
¾ cup butter (soft)
1 ½ cups of sugar

Mix all ingredients in a saucepan. Heat slowly until the mixture almost boils.
Pour over the pancakes and serve. If you really want to go all out, add a small
 scoop of vanilla ice cream on the plate.

The Patty Duke Show theme song touted that a hot dog made Patty Lane "lose control." But Patty Duke enjoyed baking. And what else would you expect from one so American…

Patty Duke's Deep Dish Apple Pie

(Serves 6-8)

1 prepared double crust pastry
Tart green cooking apples, enough to make 7-7 ½ c. peeled and sliced
1/3 c. white sugar
1/3 c. light brown sugar
2 tbsp. flour
Pinch salt
1 tsp. ground cinnamon or ½ tsp. ground mace
3 tbsp. sweet butter cut in small pieces
Juice and grated rind of 1 lemon
½ c. dairy sour cream or heavy cream
1 egg yolk mixed with 1 tbsp. water
Whipped cream or ice cream or a good aged Cheddar cheese, sliced

Roll out half the dough and line a deep, 9 inch pie plate; set aside.
Wrap remainder of dough in aluminum foil and refrigerate until ready to roll out.
Peel and slice apples.
Combine white sugar, brown sugar, flour, salt, spices. Coat apples with mixture.
Add butter, lemon juice and rind.
Fill lower crust with apple mixture. Spread sour cream over apples.
Roll out top crust; cut steam vent.
Attach top crust to lower crust, sealing edges. Brush top with egg yolk-water mixture.
Bake in preheated 375 degree F. oven for 50 minutes.
Serve warm with whipped cream, ice cream or a slice of Cheddar cheese per serving.

NOTE: The secret to my pie is the selection of good, tart eating apples. If apples are not flavorful, sprinkle with lemon or lime juice to bring out natural flavor of the fruit.

Riverboat

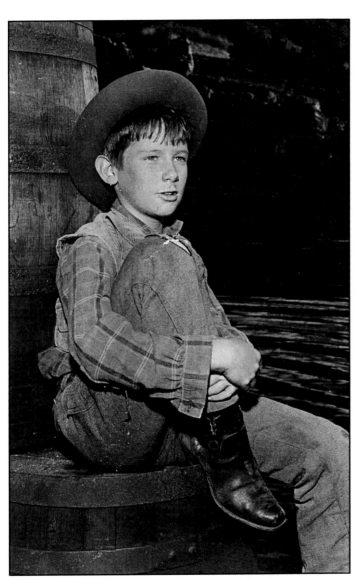

Riverboat was a Western series about a captain and his crew of The Enterprise, a riverboat in the 1830s and '40s, traveling the Mississippi, Missouri and Ohio Rivers where they meet an interesting cast of characters which includes many beautiful women.

Dan Duryea was replaced as captain after two episodes by Darren McGavin. Michael McGreevey was cast in seventeen episodes as cabin boy Chip Kessler. Crew member, Burt Reynolds, in his television debut, shot 20 episodes before clashes with McGavin caused him to be replaced by Noah Beery, Jr. The show ran for two seasons from September 13, 1959 to January 2, 1961 with a total of 44 episodes.

Michael McGreevey

Michael McGreevey began his professional career at the age of seven, appearing in *The Girl Most Likely* in 1958 with Jane Powell, the first of 18 films he would act in over the next 20 years. Michael also appeared in over 100 television shows, including stints as a series regular on *Riverboat*, Burt Reynolds' first show; and guest-star appearances on such acclaimed series as *Naked City*, *Route 66* and three two-part specials for *Walt Disney's Wonderful World of Color*.

At 18, he enrolled at UCLA while continuing his professional acting career, starring opposite Kirk Douglas, Robert Mitchum and Sally Field in *The Way West*, with David

Niven in *The Impossible Years* and alongside Richard Widmark and Lena Horne in *Death of a Gunfighter*, as well as guest-starring in numerous television shows like *Mod Squad*), *Love, American Style* and made-for-TV movies including *If Tomorrow Comes* with Patty Duke.

Graduating from UCLA Film School with honors, he set his sights on one day moving behind the camera to write, direct, and produce while continuing to work as an actor. He made guest-star appearances on acclaimed television series like *The Waltons*; and co-starred opposite Kurt Russell in a series of very successful movies for Disney: *The Computer Wore Tennis Shoes, Now You See Him, Now You Don't, Snowball Express* and *The Strongest Man in the World*.

Mike with Kurt Russell in *The Computer Wore Tennis Shoes*

During all his free time, he wrote. His first professional writing assignment was a collaboration with his award-winning father, John McGreevey, developing a three-hour movie for television about the Kennedy assassination entitled *Ruby and Oswald* in 1978. A truly monumental television event, *Ruby and Oswald* was a ratings winner as well as a critical success. Michael continued writing on his own, branching out into series television, working on such shows as *The Waltons* with creator Earl Hamner Jr., *Palmerstown, U.S.A.* with Alex Haley and Norman Lear, *Quincy M.E.* and many others. Michael was nominated for an Emmy award for his teleplay of the ABC Afterschool Specials: *The Celebrity and the Arcade Kid.* What started out as a freelance assignment writing one episode of *Fame*, the NBC series based on the popular film, turned into three seasons (72 episodes) as writer, story editor and eventually producer. Having written more episodes than anyone else, Michael was the obvious choice to write the last *Fame* episode, bringing the award-winning series to an end.

After *Fame,* Michael needed a break from the grind of series television and returned to writing long-form television, developing movies and mini-series for all the networks, including NBC's highest rated movie of the '94 season, *Bonanza: The Return*. Michael returned to series television as the Supervising Producer of *High Tide* for the '95-'96 season and then assumed the same duties on the syndicated series, *Tarzan: The Epic Adventures*, completing 22 episodes for the '96-'97 season. He realized another life-long dream by directing one of the episodes.

Having been bitten by the directing bug, Michael immediately took on another assignment, helming three episodes of the Fox Network's children series, *Mowgli: The New Adventures of the Jungle Book*. The producers were so pleased with his work on this demanding action/ adventure series that they asked him to direct an independent feature based on the Kipling books, *Jungle Book: Lost Treasure*, starring Gary Collins and Michael Beck. Immediately after completing the film, McGreevey returned to television, executive-producing as well as writing and directing 26 one-hour episodes of the syndicated series *Born Free*, a continuation of the very popular movie based on Joy Adamson's extraordinary work with the lioness, Elsa, in Africa. Since finishing the series, Michael has co-writtenan action\ thriller television movie and series pilot, *Endangered*, and co-wrote the script for a big-

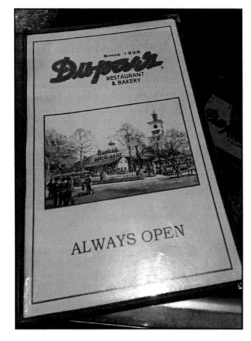

Don't know what I'm going to do now that DuPars (Studio City) closed. I guess I'll just have to drive to Hollywood to the DuPars in Farmers Market."

budget adaptation of the L. Frank Baum classic, *The Life and Adventures of Santa Claus.*

He is presently developing an original screenplay, *13 Weeks*, a romantic comedy about working in series television, and shooting three documentaries entitled *Aging Without Symptoms*, *Welcome to Eden*, and *The Face of America*. After more than 60 years in show business, Mike shows no signs of slowing down.

"My favorite food as a kid was the Patty-Melt at DuPars. I always loved when I got a job on a show that shot at Four Star Studios (CBS Radford today) because it meant that I could have lunch at DuPars in Studio City which was only a couple blocks away from the Studio. Over the years, I have continued to go to DuPars—and I always get the Patty-Melt.

"My favorite meal as an adult is my wife's Beef Stroganoff (with a nod to Better Homes and Gardens Heritage Cookbook). Debbie and I have been married 40 years and I think her Beef Stroganoff is the main reason our marriage has lasted so long. Beef Stroganoff... and the fact that she's the most amazing woman I've ever met!

McGreevey's Beef Stroganoff

(Serves 4 or 5)

1 pound beef sirloin steak, cut in thin strips
1 tablespoon all-purpose flour
1/2 teaspoon salt
2 tablespoons butter or margarine
1 3-ounce can sliced mushrooms, drained
1/2 cup chopped onion
1 clove garlic, minced
2 tablespoon butter or margarine
3 tablespoons all-purpose flour
1 tablespoon tomato paste
1 101/2-ounce can condensed beef broth
1 cup dairy sour cream
2 tablespoons dry white wine
Hot buttered noodles

Coat beef strips with mixture of 1 tablespoon flour and salt.
In a skillet, brown beef strips quickly in 2 tablespoons butter or margarine.
Add mushrooms, onion, and garlic; cook till onion is crisp-tender, 3 to 4 minutes.
Remove meat and mushrooms from pan.
Add 2 tablespoons butter or margarine to pan drippings; blend in 3 tablespoons flour.
Add tomato paste.
Stir in broth. Cook and stir over medium heat till thickened and bubbly.
Return meat and mushrooms to skillet.
Stir in sour cream and dry white wine; cook till heated through. (Do not boil.)
Serve over noodles."

Twilight Zone

The Twilight Zone sprang from the brilliant mind of Rod Serling; and was a success from the start. It explores opening the door to a "fifth dimension," vast, timeless and… "somewhere between science and superstition, between the pit of man's fears and the summit of his knowledge…the dimension of imagination… we call *The Twilight Zone.*" Compelling episodes run the gamut from science fiction to fantasy to the macabre. The original series ran on CBS for five seasons from 1959 to 1964 with 156 episodes. Many child actors guested on this series including Veronica Cartwright, Bill Mumy and Morgan Brittany.

Morgan Brittany

Morgan Brittany has been an actress almost her entire life. She has worked with such legendary stars as Rosalind Russell, Natalie Wood, Lucille Ball, Bob Hope, and Henry Fonda among many others. She has been directed by some of Hollywood's most prestigious directors like Hitchcock, Mervyn LeRoy, John Schlessinger, and Mark Rydell. 2020 marked her 63rd year as a performer in Hollywood.

Although best known for her role as Katherine Wentworth, the sophisticated but maniacal sister of Pam Ewing on *Dallas,* Morgan's career has spanned the decades. From her role as Baby June in *Gypsy* in 1962 to *The Birds, Marnie,* and *Yours, Mine and Ours,* she has enjoyed a wide variety of roles.

Morgan's career began at the age of 5 under her real name, Suzanne Cupito, when she appeared with Lloyd Bridges in the TV series *Sea Hunt.* During the '60s, she starred in over 100 television shows like *Outer Limits, Gunsmoke, The Andy Griffith Show, Lassie, Playhouse 90, My Three Sons,* and notably in three episodes of *Twilight Zone.* In 1966, she became a member of Richard Boone's repertory company.

After attending college at Cal State University at Northridge, Morgan preformed a brief stint in Vegas as a dancing partner to the great Gene Kelly in *Gene Kelly's Wonderful World of Girls.*

Afterward, she moved to New York in pursuit of a modeling career. Within a month, she had landed 6 national commercials and became the spokesperson for Ultra-Bright Toothpaste, Avon Cosmetics, Ford, Max Factor and L'Oreal Cosmetics. She was also the "Milk Girl" for the CA Milk Advisory Board. Her modeling career took her to the Orient where she became the face of Kanebo Cosmetics in Japan, Korea, and much of the Far East.

She returned to the US three years later and moved into feature films such as *Gable and Lombard* and *Day of the Locust*. In both films, she portrayed a young Vivien Leigh, a role she would repeat in the NBC mini-series *Moviola —The Scarlett O'Hara War* which also starred Tony Curtis.

Her many *Movie of the Week* credits include playing Mrs. Howard Hughes in *The Amazing Howard Hughes* with Tommy Lee Jones. She portrayed Alice Glass, Lyndon Johnson's infamous mistress in *LBJ: The Early Years* with Randy Quaid and the silent screen's "It" Girl, Clara Bow in *The Dream Merchants*.

She has also starred in her own ABC TV series for Aaron Spelling, *Glitter.* Her TV credits include: *Melrose Place, Sabrina the Teenaged Witch, The Nanny, Married with Children, L.A. Law, Perry Mason Mysteries, Murder She Wrote,* and guesting on many more. She also had the honor of traveling with Bob Hope for many of his TV specials.

Morgan has been married for 37 years to director/stunt coordinator, Jack Gill. They have two children, Katie, an actress and Cody, a composer/musician. Morgan and Jack are active supporters of the March of Dimes for more than 20 years. They have raised more than $10 million for them.

Morgan has been honored by Big Brothers/Big Sisters of Southern CA and received a lifetime achievement award from the Southern CA Motion Picture Council.

Recently, her career has shifted back to the theater and her musical roots. She recently starred in the 35th Anniversary tour of *Mame* in the title role. She also toured in *Crazy for You* and starred as Maria in *The Sound of Music*.

Morgan is also very active in the protection of young children in the motion picture industry. She was on the Screen Actors Guild Board for three years and is a member of the Young Performers Committee. She also sits on the Advisory Boards for the CDC's Business/Labor Responds to AIDS program and an advisory member for the Entertainment Industry Council. Politically active over the last few years, she is an outspoken conservative Republican, appearing on many radio and TV shows supporting Conservative candidates and traveling for John McCain in the 2008 election. She sits on the Advisory Board for the Hollywood Congress of Republicans. In 2009 she began appearing on Fox News' *Hannity Show* where she was a member of the Great American Panel. Her current passion is supporting veterans groups, and bringing public awareness of the needs of our troops past and present.

Today, Morgan is one of two leading journalists for *Politichicks.com* a conservative media website for patriots across the country. She is also a contributing columnist for Townhall Finance and appears on CNBC, FOX, and *The Blaze* discussing the economy. She released two books with her Politichicks partner, *What Women Really Want* and *Politichicks: A Clarion Call to Political Activism.*

She intends to keep active whether behind or in front of the camera and will continue to fight for Conservative values, America's military veterans and the greatness of America.

"One of my favorite places to go when I was a child was a little restaurant called The Hot Dog Show. I think there were a number of locations around Los Angeles, but there were two of them that I remember; one was in Toluca Lake and the other right next door to The Tail of the Cock restaurant in Sherman Oaks. The Hot Dog Show had my favorite type of food, quick and easy hot dogs! I remember always ordering the same thing, a number 3 - Chihuahua. It was a delicious hot dog smothered in chili and onions cradled in a soft hot dog bun. That would be paired with an icy cold Coca Cola. Heaven!

I have a rather bittersweet story connected to the Toluca Lake restaurant, and I remember it well. It was in the early '60s, and I was celebrating my birthday. My mother asked if I wanted to have a little party with some friends and I immediately asked if we could all meet up at The Hot Dog Show.

She said okay and we made plans, inviting about 8 children for a party the next week. I had booked a Kool-Aid commercial being filmed at Cascade Studios in Hollywood, and my agent said that it was on the day that my party was scheduled. Being a child actor, we all assumed that the day would end early and I could make the 4:00 p.m. party. Well, we were working with a kangaroo on set that day and he was not being cooperative; so the day stretched longer than we thought. At 5:30, I was finally released; and we hurried over to the party. When we arrived at 6:00, the party was over. There were balloons and a half-eaten cake, party favors scattered around, but no kids. They had come, had a great time and then had to go home for school the next day. Fortunately, I didn't take it too hard. I knew the ups and downs of being a working actor and realized even at that early age, that work came first. It was disappointing, but I sat down, the hot dog guy took my order and brought me the best Chihuahua thatI had ever eaten!

I have great memories of my childhood, and this was one has a special place in my heart.

My roots are deeply embedded in the southern part of this country. My family is from Georgia, North Carolina, and Virginia so I know southern food! One of my all-time favorite meals is something that I make for my family all of the time.

Morgan's Smothered Pork Chops

(Serves 6)

6 3/4 inch thick pork chops
1 tablespoon brown sugar
1/2 teaspoon salt
1/4 teaspoon pepper
Flour—all purpose
Hot bacon drippings
1 medium onion, peeled and sliced
1 medium green pepper, cored, seeded and sliced
1 lemon, sliced and seeded

Combine the sugar, salt and pepper.
Liberally rub the mixture onto both sides of the pork chops.
Coat the chops with flour.
Fry them in 1/4 in hot bacon drippings in a large heavy skillet (I use cast iron) until they are browned on both sides,
then remove them from the skillet and set aside.
Add onion and green pepper and sauté until slightly tender.
Return the chops to the skillet.
Add the lemon slices and water to come about 1/2 inch up the sides of the pan.
Cover and simmer over low heat 1 to 1 1/2 hours or until they are very tender.
Add additional water if necessary.
Serve with side dish of fried okra and jalapeno cornbread and you will have a feast!"

1970s

The turmoil of the 1960s went a long way in toughening up the country: political assassinations, the fight for civil rights, Vietnam, and just months into 1970, the student shootings at Kent State. The innocence and naivete of the '50s seemed worlds away. Viewers now expected more reality-based shows, no matter when they took place. Dramas like *Family*, *Little House on the Prairie* and *The Waltons* dealt with life and death issues.

Ku Fu conjured up the Old West with a new spiritual twist. Children escaped to the *Land of the Lost* or figured things out for themselves with help from *The Hardy Boys*. Even as we laughed at *The Odd Couple* and *The Brady Bunch*, their plots dealt with divorce and blended families. And everyone—black and white—laughed at the antics of the black ensemble cast of *What's Happening*!!

The Brady Bunch

The Brady Bunch tells the story of a lovely lady with three daughters who falls in love with a great guy with three sons; and the joys and challenges of living in a large blended family. Florence Henderson and Robert Reed starred as Carol and Mike Brady. Girls Marcia, Jan and Cindy were played by Maureen McCormick, Eve Plumb and Susan Olsen. Boys Greg, Peter and Bobby were played by Barry Williams, Christopher Knight and Mike Lookinland. The inimitable Ann B. Davis shone as housekeeper and cook, Alice. The series aired 117 episodes over five seasons from September 26, 1969, to March 8, 1974 on ABC. Its popularity increased during decades of syndication, raising it to iconic status.

Barry Williams

Born and raised in Southern California, Barry William Blenkhorn began his career as an 11-year-old studying acting and music with other young artists. With his first job on television's *Run for Your Life*, Barry became Barry Williams and launched himself into a diversified and distinguished show business career that has spanned over 5 decades. Early television credits include *Dragnet, The FBI, It Takes a Thief, Gomer Pyle, USMC, The Mod Squad, Marcus Welby, MD,* and *Mission Impossible.* Then came *The Brady Bunch,* where he was cast as America's most reliable big brother, Greg.

The Brady Bunch has enjoyed unprecedented success spawning subsequent sequels, movies, a cartoon show, a variety show called *The Brady Bunch Hour,* specials and even another series titled simply *The Bradys.* Barry was the recipient of the Young Artist Foundation Former Child Star Lifetime Achievement Award in 1989. Immediately following his years with *The Brady Bunch,* Barry moved to New York and won the title role in the Broadway musical *Pippin.* He created the role of the First National Touring Company and returned to New York to join the cast on Broadway. This launched an extensive career in Musical Theatre with over 85 productions including Broadway, Broadway National Tours, Regional Theatre and Performing Arts Centers. Starring roles include; *Romance/Romance, City of Angels, The Music Man, Sound of Music, Oklahoma!, Grease, West Side Story* and many others.

Barry wrote his autobiography, *Growing Up Brady: I Was a Teenage Greg* which stayed on the New York Times bestseller list for more than six months. Williams then Executive Produced *Growing Up Brady* into a two-hour TV movie for NBC. He hosted *The Barry Williams Show* on radio for 5 years as a DJ on satellites' SiriusXM. Barry has recorded several CDs and performed all over the world. In 2013 he starred in the SyFy television movie *Bigfoot.* Barry produced and wrote a live variety musical show; *'70s Music Celebration! Starring Barry Williams* which ran for 6 years in Branson, MO. Williams also wrote, co-produced and starred in 3 USO Christmas Shows, touring the world and bringing USA entertainment to our troops overseas. Currently, Mr. Williams resides in Branson, MO. with his wife Tina. He continues to sing, act and perform with no early retirement plans. He is a member of the musical trio *Barry Williams and The Traveliers.*

Barry Williams' Grilled Cheese Switcheroo

"Growing up, I loved the grilled cheese sandwich, but I loved it with lunch meat on one side—it could be sliced beef or ham on sourdough bread—the only way to make it—toasted with butter on the outside. My mom used to make that, and then she trained me, which was very wise of her. It got so that I used to ask her, 'Hey, can I go make myself lunch?'

When Tina and I started dating, one of the first things we realized was that we shared a love of cooking. I love the preparation part. She loves the heat it up stuff. The recipe here was a mutual effort. We love the Mediterranean diet – you know, fresh everything. We were looking for a way to spice up chicken strips. So we started picking things we liked. It was a wonderful experiment over several weeks: a little more of this, a little more of that, and we arrived as close to a way to do it that we could write it down. We don't measure anything; we just eyeball it.

Barry and Tina's Mediterranean Chicken

(Serves 2)

Preheat oven to 400 degrees.
In a bowl place enough Olive Oil to drench the chicken, Chopped Parsley or Parsley Flakes, Chopped Basil or Basil Flakes, black pepper to taste
3 cloves of fresh Minced Garlic and fresh-squeezed juice from 1/2 a lemon
One small pack of chicken strips—8 to 10.
Place chicken strips in bowl and coat all sides of chicken. Place Chicken in Glass baking dish.
Don't discard the Olive Oil and Herbs in the bowl.
Chop 1/2 Yellow Onion and enough Grape Tomatoes, Black Olives, Green Olives and Capers to cover the top of Chicken. Drizzle remaining Olive Oil and Herbs over the top. Bake for 20 minutes.
Place your favorite Shredded Cheese on top of the chicken and bake 2 more minutes or until cheese is melted. Serve with Basmati or Jasmine Rice.
Buon appetito!"

Family

Family was a ground-breaking drama that starred Sada Thompson and James Broderick as Kate and Doug Lawrence, a happily-married couple living in Pasadena, California with their three children: Meredith Baxter Birney as Nancy, Gary Frank as Willie and Kristy McNichol as Letitia, nicknamed Buddy. An adopted daughter played by Quinn Cummings joined the cast in 1978. Storylines were topical and controversial This critically acclaimed show, known for superb performances and controversial subject matter, was nominated for more than two dozen awards. It aired on ABC from March 9, 1976 – June 25, 1980 for a total of 86 episodes in 5 seasons.

Kristy McNichol

Kristy McNichol is best known for her moving portrayal of "Buddy" in the hit series *Family*, which ran for 5 seasons from 1976-1980. She wowed audiences and critics alike with the depth of emotion she was able to bring to the role at such a young age, winning two Emmys, a Critics Choice Award and a Golden Globe nomination in the process.

Kristy was born in 1962 in Los Angeles. She appeared with her brother, Jimmy, in commercials; and later, on her own, in guest on series like *Starsky & Hutch, The Bionic Woan, Love American Style* and *The Love Boat*. Her first stint as a series regular came in the role of Patricia Apple in the short-lived CBS television series *Apple's Way* in 1974.

During her career, Kristy has been fortunate to work with industry legends. Her many film credits include Alan Pakula's *Dream Lover*, Samuel Fuller's *White Dog*, and Neil Simon's *Only When I Laugh* with Marsha Mason which earned her another Golden Globe nomination.

Kristy began her feature film career in the Burt Reynolds comedy *The End* and went on to star with Dennis Quaid and Mark Hamill in *The Night the Lights Went Out in Georgia, Two Moon Junction* with Louise Fletcher and *The Pirate Movie* with Christopher Atkins.

Her critically acclaimed starring role in *Little Darlings* opposite Tatum O'Neal brought her a People's Choice Award in 1980. Kristy also performed voice characters in several animated TV series, including *Extreme Ghostbusters* and Steven Spielberg's animated *Invasion America*.

And speaking of voice work, Kristy is also a singer. Albums include the soundtracks for both *The Pirate Movie* and *The Night the Lights Went Out in Georgia* and the "Kristy and Jimmy McNichol" album for RCA Records.

Her outstanding athletic ability is memorable in the ABC special *Battle of the Network Stars* and NBC's *Challenge of the Network Stars*. And the Mattel Toy Company even created a doll for her! Her television movie credits are endless, including *Women of Valor, Like Mom, Like Me, Summer of My German Soldier, Love, Mary*. And from 1988 to 1992, she co-starred in the series *Empty Nest* with Richard Mulligan and Dinah Manoff. She left the show in 1992 but returned for its final episode in 1995. It was her last on-screen performance. In June 2001, Kristy announced her retirement from acting.

Her publicist released this statement:

"A lot of people have wondered what I've been up to. I retired from my career after 24 years. My feeling was that it was time to play my biggest part – myself! I must say that it has been the best thing that ever happened to me. So many fans are disappointed that I'm not currently acting; however, some may not realize that the process I'm in at this time is necessary and vital for my personal happiness and well-being."

"My favorite food as a child was spaghetti…which is really all about the sauce. I'm a meat sauce girl and I have been using this recipe which I got from family for close to 45 years!

Kristy's Childhood Spaghetti Sauce

2 lbs ground lean beef
1 small can of mushroom slices
and pieces
1 onion

garlic powder
1 bell pepper
salt and pepper

2 cans of whole tomatoes
    Italian seasoning
2 8 oz cans of tomato sauce
1 2 oz can of tomato paste

Brown beef
Chop and sauté small onion and add to beef.
Chop and sauté bell pepper and add small amount.

Add whole tomatoes, tomato sauce, tomato paste,
2 oz. of water and mushroom slices
and pieces. Season to taste with garlic powder,
salt, pepper and Italian seasoning.
Simmer   at least one hour. Ladle over prepared pasta.

As an athlete and someone who has a healthy lifestyle, I looked for a long time for an alternative for one of my big weaknesses—French fries. I finally found it in sweet potato fries which I bake. This is my favorite recipe for them. I'm happy to have the opportunity to share it with more people."

Kristy's Homemade Baked Sweet Potato Fries

(4 servings)

4 medium sweet potatoes
3 Tbl olive oil
¾ Tsp kosher salt
½ Tsp fresh ground black pepper

Heat oven to 450°

Line two baking sheets with aluminum foil and put them in the oven to heat
Scrub the potatoes. You can leave the skin on which is the way I prefer them or you can peel them.
Cut potatoes into ½ inch sticks and put in large bowl
Add olive oil, salt and pepper and toss.
Pour them onto the baking sheets in one layer and not too close together or they won't brown.
Cook for 25 minutes.

Notes:
Depending on how thick you cut your fries, baking time will vary.
You may use pink Himalayan salt in place of kosher salt.
Great with a little coconut sugar sprinkled on top.
You may also sprinkle a touch of Trader Joe's 21 Salute—so yummy!!

The Hardy Boys

The Hardy Boys was no stranger to TV. This ABC series was the fourth adaptation of this popular mystery series about two amateur detective brothers, Frank and Joe Hardy. This version starred Parker Stevenson and Shaun Cassidy and aired as *The Hardy Boys/Nancy Drew Mysteries* with Pamela Sue Martin and later Janet Louise Johnson as the teen girl sleuth. In season one, the series featured *The Hardy Boys* one week and *Nancy Drew* the next. The second season focused more on *The Hardy Boys*, with Nancy Drew appearing in just a few episodes with the brothers.

Half-way through the season, Martin quit and was replaced by Johnson. The third season, *Nancy Drew* was dropped completely and the title changed to simply *The Hardy Boys*. A total of 46 episodes were shot from January 30, 1977 to January 14, 1979.

Parker Stevenson's mom was a Broadway actress who also appeared in numerous television commercials. She took him to a filming session when he was 5 years old, which led to him making two small television appearances. He returned to commercials at 14 and made more than 120 of them. But Parker had no intention of being an actor. Architecture was his love, that and photography. He majored in architecture at Princeton. After graduation, he moved to Los Angeles, where film work came easily. His first role was in the notable *A Separate Peace*, followed by *Our Time* and *Lifeguard* among others.

But it is as amateur sleuth Frank Hardy in *The Hardy Boys* that Parker is best remembered. Teamed with younger brother, Joe played by Shaun Cassidy, the fictional brothers solved crimes while Parker and Shaun stole the hearts of millions of teens. He followed that success with roles in *Falcon Crest*, *Melrose Place*, and *Probe*.

Parker's many TV movie appearances include *North and South II*, *Shooting Stars*, *Are You Lonesome Tonight? Not of This Earth*, *All the Rivers Run II* and *Showroom*.

Then came the role of Craig Pomeroy in the 'most successful series in the history of television,' the runaway hit *Baywatch*. Parker and David Hasselhoff heated up screens around the world, but as the series progressed, Parker found himself moving behind the camera. As a director, he worked on multiple episodes of the show as well as *Baywatch Nights, Melrose Place, Savannah,* and *Models Inc.* Parker provided voice narration for the National Geographic series *Hunter/Hunted* and has done commercial voiceover spots for Sylvania, Macintosh, Blue Cross/Blue Shield, AMD, Calloway and Intel, to name but a few. Of his many projects, he is most proud of having exec produced and starred in the two-hour TV epic *Avalon: Adventures of the Abyss.*

Today, in addition to roles on television and film, Parker continues his work behind the camera as a Fine Art photographer which takes him around the globe. He currently lives in Marina Del Rey, CA. with his wife, Lisa, a chef!

"I so clearly remember standing on an old fashioned milk crate to be tall enough to look down into the bowl to whisk the eggs, milk, and sugar. The sweet smell of the heating butter in the pan let me know it was time to drop the dripping bread onto the heat. I loved seeing the browned edges appear and the anticipation of the warmth and taste of the first bite drenched in maple syrup. I had the greatest sense of achievement when it was all done.

Parker's Childhood "Fav French Toast"

(Serves 2)

4 Slices 'Wonder Bread'
4 Large Eggs
¼ cup whole milk
1 Tsp granulated Sugar
4 Tbs Butter
Confectionary Sugar for garnish
Pure Maple Syrup

In a large bowl, whisk the eggs, milk, and sugar until combined.
Heat a large non-stick sauté pan over medium heat. Add butter.
Dip each slice of bread in egg mixture and place in pan. Brown bread on each side.
Remove bread and sprinkle confectionary sugar over the top.
Pour maple syrup on toast. Enjoy.

I am not a foodie. I often eat just to get fuel into my body to be able to press on with whatever I am immersed in. I get lost for days editing photographs or researching a project. My refrigerator is often stocked with little more than string cheese, peanut butter, juice and coffee. Eventually I realize I haven't eaten anything decent in days. This is when I turn to my 'Emergency Pasta.' I keep the staples of the ingredients in my pantry so that I only need to get the ground meat. I love reconnecting with the fun of creating something not only better for me but truly delicious.

Parker's "Emergency Pasta"

(Serves 4)

1 Lb Gound Veal
2 Tbs Minced Garlic
2 Tbs Fennel Seeds
¼ Cup Sambuca
1 Tbs Red Chili Flakes
2 Tbs Olive Oil
2 Tbs Tomato Paste
1 Qt Chicken Stock
1 Lb Box of Pasta (Penne)
Fresh Basil
Grated Parmesan Cheese
Salt & Pepper

In a bowl combine the veal, garlic, fennel seeds, Sambuca, & Chili Flakes.
Heat a large Saute Pan, add 2Tbs Olive Oil, and the 'gound meat' mixture.
Saute and break up the meat mixture till golden brown (approx. 10 min.).
Add Tomato Paste and stir for I min.
Add Chicken Stock, stir, and reduce liquid by half.
Cook the Pasta of your choice (I love penne) per the packaging instructions
Drain and add to the Meat Sauce
Garnish with Fresh Basil and/or grated parmesan.
Add Salt /pepper to taste. Enjoy."

Kung Fu

Kung Fu, a martial arts Western drama series, starred David Carradine as Kwai Chang Caine, a Shaolin monk armed only with his skill in Kung Fu traveling the American Old West in search of his half-brother. Flashbacks reveal Caine's childhood spiritual training in the monastery with his teachers, the blind Master Po (Keye Luke) and Master Chen Ming Kan (Philip Ahn). The young Caine, Grasshopper, is played by Radames Pera. Nominated for more than two dozen awards during its three-year run from 1972 to 75, the series produced a total of 63 episodes.

Radames Pera

Radames Pera's path begins with his name. Radames rhymes with 'hippopotamus' and Pera with 'hurrah!' His grandparents—whom he never met—were opera buffs. They named his father, Radames for the general who falls in love with Aida. Their last name (opera without the "O") is the word for pear in both Italian and Spanish, their heritage.

Radames was three years old when he and his mom moved from his birthplace of New York to Hollywood in 1963 so that she could pursue an acting career. But it was Radames who ended up being discovered five years later by one of the top movie directors of the 1950s and '60s, Daniel Mann, who cast him as Anthony Quinn's son in *A Dream of Kings*. Radames' work showed great emotional depth, and he began working steadily, mostly in television: *The Cosby Show, Family Affair, Cannon, Night Gallery, The Waltons, Lassie, Hawaii Five-O*. The producers of a new series called *Kung Fu* grabbed him up in 1972 to portray Grasshopper, the younger version of the show's star, David Carradine. The series garnered ardent fans during its three-year run; and today it has acquired cult status.

Radames followed that with a guest role in *The Six Million Dollar Man*. Two years later, he was cast in another series, *Little House on the Prairie* as John Sanderson Edwards, the writer fiancée of *Mary Ingalls*. After *Little House,* a few films followed, of note *Very Like a Whale* with Alan Bates and *Red Dawn* with Charlie Sheen; and some television. But there was no denying that the work had slowed. Radames drew on his knowledge of electronics and love of design to start his own business designing and installing home theaters and residential sound systems first in Los Angeles, then Portland and then in Austin. His love of travel and adventure continues. Radames now lives in France with his wife and daughter, and where he has just completed his memoir.

"As with most Macrobiotic practitioners (of which I am not one) who are notorious for having a complete opposite sweet indulgence occasionally, my blast from the past would be an old family friend's recipe for Lemon Cream Cheese Pie-Fondly But Not Completely Remembered

Lemon Cream Cheese Pie

This starts with a butter, graham cracker and pecan crust, a one-inch layer of silky, lightly vanilla'd cream cheese and a thin, quarter-inch top layer of lightly lemon-infused cream cheese.

Divine. Sadly, years ago, I misplaced the exact recipe that Jennifer Lee gave me, but I'm probably better off without it.

It's going to seem corny, what with my signature child-acting role and all, but nothing quite satisfies me like a simple bowl of pressure-cooked whole grain brown rice. You see, my late mom was once a practicing Macrobiotic for years before my Kung Fu gig.

In fact, when I was one year of age lying in the French hospital where I was wasting away with an "incurable" intestinal disease, my mother asked the nurses to bottle feed me a cooked-down puree of this very grain. They accommodated her as a last resort. Then, much to the raised eyebrows and shrugging shoulders of the pediatric staff, my mother carried me out less than a week later completely free of the unknown malady. Now, as a middle-aged man living in France again, I turn to the perfect solace of brown rice as a balance to all of the baguettes, cheeses, and sauces that are way too easy to overindulge in here.

How Radames Eats Rice

These days I'll mix in a little freshly cut sea asparagus when I find some at a farmer's market on the coast or finely chopped scallion marinated in lemon juice and salt. When those garnishes are unavailable, "the classics" are to sprinkle on a little gomasio (ground toasted sesame seeds and sea salt), or when near a Japanese food market, as city folk on the U.S. West Coast are lucky to have, a couple umeboshi (salt plums) mixed into the bowl. Satisfying, nourishing, guilt-free."

Land of the Lost

Land of the Lost, a children's adventure series, was produced by the legendary Sid and Marty Krofft, It follows the adventures of Rick Marshall (Spencer Milligan) and his children Will and Holly played by Wesley Eure and Kathy Coleman who fight for survival in a time warp inhabited by dinosaurs and other weird creatures, hoping to get back to their own world. It ran on NBC for three seasons and 43 episodes from September 7, 1974 – December 4, 1976. Continual airing in syndication has earned it cult status.

Wesley Eure

As Will Marshall on *Land of the Lost*, Wesley Eure ran for his life from all kinds of prehistoric creatures. After he left the set for the day, he ran for his life for an entirely different reason.

"I was born in Baton Rouge, Louisiana, and raised in Hattiesburg, Mississippi, so my family was Southern through and through.

When I made my way to NY at the age of 17 to start my professional career, my first job was understudying Ariel in Shakespeare's *The Tempest*. On the first day of rehearsal at the Manhattan Club, I read my first lines. "All hail, great master! Grave sir, hail! I come to answer thy best pleasure, be it to flyyyyyyy, (fly) to swiiiiiim (swim), to diiiiiiive (dive) into the fiiiiiiire (fire)

The horrified staff of Julliard School of Music, who were producing the play, yelled in chorus, "Not on our stage!!!"

My Southern accent was so thick they assigned to me a voice teacher, inguist, Liz Smith, for the entire nine-month run of the show to get rid of my accent! So my twang was lost forever unless, of course, I have too many Margaritas! Then the boy from the Deep South reappears!

In 1973, David Cassidy was threatening to leave *The Partridge Family*. Producers cast Wesley as a neighbor who would take over as lead singer in the family band, but Cassidy stayed.

In 1974, Wesley auditioned and won the part of Mike Horton on NBC's *Days of Our Lives*. At the same time, he was cast by Sid and Marty Kroft as Will Marshall on the Saturday morning kids show, *Land of the Lost*. Eure, 23 at the time, shot both shows simultaneously for the three-year run of *LOTL*, escaping from dinosaurs as a 16-year-old trapped in a time warp then dashing across Los Angeles to immerse himself in the melodrama and emotional crises as a 20-something in the soap opera. Wesley continued on *Days* until 1981.

Remarkably creative, Wesley is also the author of five books, the developer of PBS' hit show, *Dragon Tales*, and the host of Nickelodeon's game show, *Finders Keepers*.

His professional acting career began at The American Shakespeare Festival in Stratford, CT. Wesley has starred in many theatre productions, including *Bus Stop* and *Butterflies are Free*.

After all of his classical training, Wesley is now known for his line from TV's classic *Land of the Lost*… "Run, Holly! Run! There's a dinosaur!"

"My favorite adult recipe is easy! You ain't Southern if you ain't got no grits and shrimp recipe! Southern seafood and grits are not only in my belly, but also in my heart and soul! Below is a recipe that is a quick version of the old standard. Feel free to spice it up more if you are adventurous like me! I have added a few suggestions to tap into your cooking creativity."

Wesley's Quick & Easy Grits and Shrimp

FIXIN'S

       3 cups chicken broth (or vegetable broth)
       1 cup uncooked quick-cooking grits
       1/2 teaspoon salt
       1/4 teaspoon freshly ground pepper
       2 tablespoons butter
       2 cups (8 ounces) shredded Cheddar cheese
       6 slices bacon, chopped
       2 pounds medium shrimp, peeled and deveined
       1 tablespoon fresh lemon or lime juice
       1 teaspoon Cajun or blackened seasoning
       2 tablespoons chopped fresh parsley
       6 green onions, chopped
       2 garlic cloves, minced

MAKIN' IT!

First step:
Bring chicken broth (or vegetable broth if you choose) to a boil over medium-high heat; stir in grits. Cook, occasionally stirring, 5 to 7 minutes or until thickened. Remove from heat; stir in salt and next 3 ingredients. Set aside and keep warm.

Second step:
Cook bacon in a large cast-iron skillet over medium-high heat 3 minutes or until crisp; remove bacon from pan.

NOTE: No Southern home is complete without a large "seasoned" cast iron skillet, but feel free to use a non-stick pan if you are from the North! LOL If you like it less spicy, please feel free to substitute 2 teaspoons Worcestershire sauce for the Cajun or blackened seasoning.

Third step:
Cook shrimp in the same pan over medium-high heat 3 minutes or until almost pink, stirring occasionally. Add lemon juice and next 4 ingredients, and cook 3 minutes. Stir in bacon.

Fourth step:
Spoon grits onto individual plates or into shallow bowls; top with shrimp mixture.
Serve immediately. And put a bottle of Louisiana's own Tabasco Sauce on the table for those who can handle a bit more fire!

ALSO: Many Southern kitchens like to really spice it up and add Andouille sausage!
If you want, take 1 pound Andouille sausage, cut into 1/4-inch slices.
Then place Andouille sausage slices in the skillet over medium heat;
fry sausage until browned, 5 to 8 minutes. Remove skillet from heat.

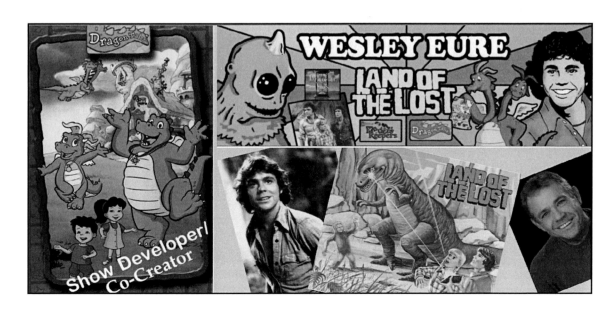

Kathy Coleman

People used to say to Kathy's mother, "You should put that kid in show business." For the mother of eight living in Massachusetts, Hollywood was a dream away. Then the clan moved to Los Angeles and it became a reality. People on the West Coast said those same words to Kathy's mom, but this time she was able to act upon them. Kathy got her first agent and her first commercial – for Shakey's Pizza—by the age of six.

"Once my mother got it through her head that Hollywood wasn't looking for the next Shirley Temple (I was Goldilocks in the Shakey's commercial), she toned down my look and the work started coming in at a steady rate. I did a number of commercials, everything from McDonald's to 409 kitchen cleaner."

At the age of 10, Kathy did two national tours singing with Mike Curb's Band, performing with everyone from Burt Bacharach to George Burns. She managed to squeeze in a guest shot on *Adam-12* between tours, but eventually, she left the band at 12 to start a new adventure.

Kathy starred on the Saturday morning series *Land of the Lost* as Holly Marshall. Her blonde braids and memorable red-and-white-check shirt became her trademark. She won the hearts of her audience with her portrayal of the courageous Holly from 1973 to 1975.

The series ran in the number one slot and lives on in reruns to this day. It even spawned a major motion picture in 2009 starring Will Ferrell.

Kathy married at 18 and more or less retired to raise two sons. In 2017, she published her memoir, entitled *Run Holly Run*, which highlights her time working on *Land of the Lost*. She signs them at comic cons and personal appearances across the country, usually with castmate Wesley Eure, a life-long friend and true brother-from-another-mother.

"As a kid, my favorite thing to eat…I'd have to say Fluturnutter Sandwich…very East Coast.

Kathy's Fluturnutter Sandwich

Take two pieces of white bread (I know, yadda, yadda, I was a kid.) Spread one with chunky peanut butter. Spread the other with marshmallow cream "Fluff." Put it together and eat with a large glass of ice-cold milk…mmmm, heaven.

'When Laurie first asked me if I wanted to give her a favorite recipe of mine for her book, I was honored. At the time I had a full plate in my life and no recipe in mind. I even tried to slide someone else's to her. I just was overwhelmed with personal issues at home. After speaking with Wesley (my costar on *LOTL*), he suggested that I give the recipe that I served to my husband every day to prolong his life during his battle with cancer.

Kathy's Smoothie for Her Sweetie

In my trusty blender I put...
    1tbsp Maca powder
    1tbsp Beet powder
    1tbsp Tumeric powder
    1tbsp Plant protein powder
    1/2 tsp Chia, Hemp and Flaxseed
    2 cups Dark Chocolate Almond milk
    1/2 cup Cherry, Carrot and
    Pomegranate juice
    1 handful of Cilantro
    2 tbsp Coconut oil
    Banana
     papaya
    strawberry
    mango
    organic blue berries
    pineapple
    jack fruit
    dragon fruit and
    on occasion, avocado.

I put in as much of all these fruits as my blender could take. I am convinced this gave me additional precious time with my sweetie. I miss you and love you, Mark!"

Little House on the Prairie

Little House on the Prairie, loosely adapted from Laura Ingalls Wilder's semi-autobiographical novels based on her youth in the American Midwest of the late 1800s, follows the lives of her simple farming family in the small town of Walnut Grove.

Michael Landon starred as Charles Ingalls with Karen Grassle as his wife, Caroline. Melissa Gilbert played Laura Ingalls; Melissa Sue Anderson was Mary Ingalls, and twins Lindsay and Sidney Greenbush played Carrie Ingalls. Others in the large cast included Victor French as long-time friend Mr. Edwards; Dean Butler as Laura's husband, Almanzo Wilder; and Alison Arngrim as spoiled brat Nellie Oleson, rival for the affections of Almanzo.

Always a top-rated series, *Little House* garnered more than 20 award nominations over its nine-year, 180-episode run from September 11, 1974 to March 21, 1983.

Alison Arngrim

New York Times Best Selling author of *Confessions of A Prairie Bitch: How I Survived Nellie Oleson and Learned to Love Being Hated*, Alison Arngrim is best known to viewers worldwide for her portrayal of the incredibly nasty Nellie Oleson on the much loved, long-running hit television series *Little House On The Prairie*. The talented actress continues to amuse audiences through her many film, television, stage, and multi-media appearances. The TV Land network honored her undying image as TV's worst bitch, by declaring her the winner of their 2006 award for "Character Most Desperately in Need of a Time Out."

Her one-woman show *Confessions of a Prairie Bitch,* which started at Club Fez in New York in 2002, has now become a worldwide phenomenon, having been performed to packed houses in New York, Los Angeles, Boston, Chicago, Philadelphia, Green Bay, San Francisco, Seattle, and in France, where Alison performs entirely in French to standing room only crowds.

As a stand-up comedian, Alison has headlined at nightclubs such as The Laugh Factory, The Comedy Store, and The Improv in Los Angeles, as well as the Laurie Beechman Theatre in New York and assorted comedy venues all across the United States and Canada.

She starred in the heartwarming gay, Christmas cult classic, *Make the Yuletide Gay*. Her other television and film appearances include *Livin' the Dream, Tinder & Grinder, The Bilderberg Club, For the Love of May* with Ru Paul and Patricia Neal, and *The Last Place On Earth* with Billy Dee Williams and Phyllis Diller. In 2007, she began her foray into French cinema in the French detective comedy, *Le Deal*.

Never one to forget her *Prairie* roots, Alison enjoys making appearances several times a year at various *Little House on the Prairie* historical sites for educational events and gatherings of fans. She has been a frequent visitor to the Laura Ingalls Wilder Museum in real life Walnut Grove, Minnesota as well as Green Bay, Wisconsin's Heritage Hills, Mumford's Genesee Country Village, Laura Ingalls Wilder Historic Home and Museum in Mansfield, Missouri and many, many others.

Alison has a long history of activism. In 1986, when her friend and *Little House* husband, Steve Tracy, passed away due to complications of HIV/AIDS, Alison immediately began volunteering at AIDS Project Los Angeles. Her duties ranged from working on the Southern California AIDS Hotline and the APLA food bank to chairing the steering committee of the volunteer speakers bureau and developing "Safer Sex" workshops. She has provided AIDS education to doctors, nurses, prison inmates, service clubs, churches, department stores and schools, written AIDS education articles for magazines, and spent seven years hosting the APLA educational cable television show, AIDS Vision.

In 1992, Joel Wachs presented Alison with a resolution by the Los Angeles City Council commending her on her work on behalf of people living with HIV and AIDS. The New York Times called her "A different breed of rainbow-draped diva."

From 1989 through 1993, she served as Program Manager at Tuesday's Child, an organization assisting children and families affected by HIV and AIDS. From 1989 through

2003 she served as both hostess and producer for the comedy stage at the AIDS Project Los Angeles Annual Summer Party on the backlot of Universal Studios where, through an evening of raucous entertainment featuring name comedians, she helped to raise hundreds of thousands of dollars for people living with HIV.

Alison currently serves as California Chair, National Spokesperson, and Founding Board Member on the National Advisory Board of The National Association to Protect Children, or PROTECT.org, fighting to give children a legal and political voice in the war against child abuse. As an activist for the improvement of child protection laws, she has spoken before the California Senate and worked on legislative and political campaigns in several states, including Virginia and New York, in addition to PROTECT's work on federal legislation in Washington, D.C.

She has appeared on numerous television news programs discussing the legal and political issues surrounding child sexual abuse and exploitation. She first came forward to tell the world about the sexual abuse she suffered in her own life during her 2004 interview on *Larry King Live.*

She is currently starring in two comedy series pilots: *Life Interrupted* as the ex-wife of commercial child star Mason Reese, with Erin Murphy (*Bewitched*) as her new wife and Dawn Wells (*Gilligan's Island*) as her mother; and *C.P.R.—Child Performers Resurrection Talent Agency,* as an ex-child star gone wrong trying to save herself and her assorted misfit cohorts by opening a talent agency.

Alison currently lives somewhere in the wilds of Tujunga with her husband of over 20 years, musician Bob Schoonover (from the rock and roll band Catahoula) and their two extraordinarily spoiled cats. She takes pride in the fact that so many people enjoyed hating her as a girl and is more than happy to allow them to do so in the future.

"Oh, I cook like a fiend! I've had recipes published in three cookbooks and am working on one of my own as we speak. I'm one of those freaks who took Home Ec three times—and liked it. So what did I love as a kid?

Truth?

Kraft Deluxe Macaroni and Cheese.

My whole family was actors. So like all actors, our income went up, went down, went away and came back. During our leaner times, macaroni and cheese became quite popular.

One Christmas, my father, a brilliant, excellent cook from whom I learned some of my best recipes, had been slaving away in the kitchen prepping for the big Christmas dinner. He knew he had a full day of cooking ahead of him. So for Christmas Eve dinner, we had some quick and easy macaroni and cheese.

Being about 5, I thought this was great! I asked my parents if we could have mac and cheese for Christmas! They immediately shared a gleeful, mischievous look..."Well, it would save a lot of time…and money," said my mother through barely suppressed giggles. There was clearly a moment of, 'do you think we could get away with it?' But they quickly dismissed the notion. They did, however, realize that they could convince me that Kraft Macaroni and Cheese was a VERY SPECIAL, possibly expensive DELICACY, to be enjoyed on VERY special occasions!

"If you're very good…we could have... MACARONI AND CHEESE!!!"

"Oh, can we??!!!!! Yeaaah!!"

A brilliant move.

I admit I still love the stuff. And I consider it a Christmas Eve tradition to eat a big bowl of it sitting under the Christmas tree!

Today, it's a different story. I have a recipe I use for "Cinnamon Chicken,"—which of course, is the infamous dinner from *Little House*. There's "regular cinnamon chicken"—and there's the "cayenne pepper version" that Laura made as revenge on Nellie!

If you saw the episode "Back to School," you know that Nellie forces poor Laura to cook cinnamon chicken for her and Almanzo so she can take credit and steal her man! Laura gets her revenge by replacing the cinnamon entirely with CAYENNE PEPPER, positively nuking Nellie and Almanzo's taste buds and sending them from the table screaming and choking.

Well, you really don't want to make THAT. But...I've created a nice cinnamon chicken, with just a HINT of spicy bad girl hotness!

Alison's Spicy Cinnamon Chicken

2 medium chicken, boneless, skinless breasts
1/4 cup milk
1/2 cup flour
2 tablespoons Cinnamon, (3 if you really like cinnamon!)
1/2 teaspoon Cayenne Pepper
Dash of salt and pepper, to taste
Olive oil
Butter or margarine
2 tablespoons liquid—water or chicken broth (or wine!)

Mix flour, Cinnamon, Cayenne Pepper, and salt and pepper. Sift together or stir thoroughly with a fork.Dip chicken breasts in milk, then dredge in flour cinnamon mixture till thoroughly coated.
Put a small amount of olive oil in a skillet and heat. (I use a non-stick, but cast iron, etc., works, as long as it comes with a tight-fitting lid).
Place coated chicken breasts in hot oil.
Brown on each side, a few minutes each.
After you've turned them and they're sizzling, add butter or margarine and the liquid.
Place lid on tightly and lower heat.

Let cook for a few minutes, until cooked through, allowing breasts to absorb liquid (and become super moist).
Serve with mashed potatoes, drizzling liquid from the pan over chicken and potatoes.

You may adjust the Cayenne amount depending on taste.
1/4 teaspoon for mild, 1/2 for a light spicy kick, a little more if you're very adventurous!"

The Odd Couple

The Odd Couple is based on the Neil Simon play about two divorced men who share a Manhattan apartment where their different lifestyles lead to conflicts. Tony Randall starred as Felix Unger, an anal neat freak while Jack Klugman starred as Oscar Madison, an inherent slob. It was both critically and publically acclaimed.

Pamelyn Ferdin appeared as Felix's teenaged daughter, Edna in three episodes in 1971-72 season. The series ran for five seasons and 114 episodes, broadcast on ABC from September 24, 1970, to March 7, 1975.

Pamelyn Ferdin

Pamelyn Ferdin, a native Angelean, was cast in her first television commercial at the age of three. She made her acting debut in film and TV at the age of four. As a child and teen, she was the hardest-working child actor of the '70s, appearing in more than 200 TV shows including memorable episodes of *Star Trek* and *The Brady Bunch*, and series such as *Lassie* and *The Paul Lynde Show.* She is still recognized as Felix Unger's daughter, Edna, from *The Odd Couple,* but it's her distinctive voice that's a dead give-away to her most famous role — as the voice of Lucy Van Pelt in *Peanuts* television specials and the movie, *A Boy Named Charlie Brown.* Pamelyn acted in more than two dozen motion pictures and made-for-TV movies and hundreds of commercials.

Despite her success, she gave up acting to attend nursing school to become a registered nurse. But it was a life-long love of animals that eventually led her to her true calling as an advocate and activist for animal rights to put an end to cruelty to animals.

"From the time I was very young, I remember feeling sorry for animals I saw or heard were mistreated. I remember, too, how I felt, as the voice of Fern in the animated movie *Charlotte's Web*, reading the wonderful words of author E. B. White about animals having personalities, and experiencing fear, anxiety, and happiness. Whether it was those I worked with on television or movie sets or my own companion animals at home, looking into their eyes, how could I deny that animals feel the same emotions we humans feel?

As an adult, I witnessed the terrible suffering of animals in factory farms and slaughterhouses. I came to understand that by eating dead animals, I was giving my consent to the exploitation and killing of innocent beings. I couldn't, in good conscience, continue to live that way. I became vegan, meaning I neither eat, wear, or use any products made from animals.

Many people hold the mistaken belief that consuming meat and other animal products is a requirement for health. In fact, a diet of animal products brings with it a vastly increased rate of disease caused by the cholesterol, fat, pesticides, and chemical additives that are part and parcel of an animal-based diet.

Also, A well-balanced vegan diet can easily provide all the nutrients we need to thrive. there is a large body of scientific evidence that demonstrates that a vegan diet is not only a viable option for people of any age, but that eating plant foods instead of animal-based foods can confer significant health benefits, including a reduction in the incidence of obesity, diabetes, high blood pressure, heart disease, stroke, and some types of cancer.

Every day, each of us has the opportunity to live our values through our food choices. If we value kindness toward animals over violence, compassion over brutality and indifference, then veganism is the only consistent expression of our values. Peace for ALL the animals with whom we share the planet!"

"As a child, my favorite food was peanut butter and jelly sandwiches. I still love them (and they're vegan!), but I also love a bowl of delicious, comforting chili. Here is a recipe for a simple, hearty, stick-to-your-ribs vegan chili. Enjoy!"

Pamelyn's Hearty Vegan Chili

(serves 8 to 10)

2 Tbsp. oil
6 garlic cloves, minced
1 cup chopped white onion
1 lb. vegan ground (I like Gardein Ultimate Beefless Ground or Yves Veggie Ground, but any crumbled veggie burgers will do)
Red pepper flakes to taste
1 Tbsp. chili powder
2 ½ tsp. cumin
1 tsp. oregano
1 bay leaf
28-oz. can diced Mexican-style tomatoes
1 Tbsp. soy sauce
1 ½ cups vegetable stock
6 oz. tomato paste
1 Tbsp. red wine vinegar
28 oz. kidney beans
16 oz. pinto beans
vegan sour cream , Daiya Cheddar Style Shreds, chopped chives (optional)

Heat the oil in a large pot over medium heat.
Add the garlic and onion and saute until softened, about 5 minutes.
Add the vegan ground, red pepper flakes, chili powder, and cumin and cook for an additional 2minutes. Add the oregano, bay leaf, tomatoes, soy sauce vegetable stock, tomato paste, and vinegar, then bring to a boil.
Lower the heat and simmer 30 minutes, stirring occasionally.
Add the beans and simmer for 15 minutes longer to heat through and blend flavors.
Add water, if necessary, or cook longer to reach desired consistency.

The Waltons

The Waltons, a dramatic series created by Earl Hamner Jr., was based on his book *Spencer's Mountain*. It chronicles the life of the family of John Walton, Jr. —Richard Thomas movingly performed John-Boy—the eldest of 7 children growing up in rural Virginia during the Great Depression and World War II from 1933 to 1946. His parents, John, Sr. and Olivia are portrayed by Ralph Waite and Michael Learned; and Grandpa and Grandma Walton by Will Geer and Ellen Corby. Sisters Mary Ellen, Erin and Elizabeth are played by Judy Norton, Mary McDonough and Kami Colter. The brothers Jason, Ben and Jim-Bob are brought to life by Jon Walmsley, Eric Scott and David W. Harper.

Recognized for the quality of both the writing and performances, *The Waltons* was nominated for more than 75 awards during its nine-year, 221-episode run from September 14, 1972 – June 4, 1981.

Judy Norton

Born in Los Angeles, Judy began acting at the age of 6, working on television in shows like *Ozzie & Harriet*, *The Tammy Grimes Show*, and *Felony Squad* before landing the role of Mary Ellen in the 1971 TV movie *The Homecoming*. The success of this Christmas special resulted in *The Waltons* TV series, which launched 13-year-old Judy to international fame. An outstanding series, *The Waltons* won many awards during its 9-year run.

Her post-*Waltons* credits include numerous *Waltons* TV movie reunions and holiday specials along with appearances on *Millenium*, *The Inspectors*, *Stargate–SG1*, *Ed*, several feature films and the mini-series *Lost Daughter*. She also appeared in a recurring role on the series, *Beggars & Choosers*, *Bluff* and *Disorganized Zone*. During season one of *Bluff*, the multi-talented Judy came on board as head writer and directed several episodes. And she co-produced, wrote and directed several episodes of *Disorganized Zone* as well.

For many years, Judy has been a member of the artistic team of Texas Family Musicals, where she regularly guests as a writer, director and performer; most recently directing productions of *A Chorus Line*, *All Shook Up*, and Red Skelton's *American Way*. In 2014, Judy wrote the original two-character show *Moments Remembered* which premiered at the Palace Theatre starring Judy and Don Most of *Happy Days* fame.

Judy is also a veteran of the stage, making her first appearance on the *"boards"* at the age of 7. She spent 8 years as the co-artistic director for 2 theatres in Canada, collaborating as a writer/director on more than 40 shows. In 2009, Judy directed the highly successful Musical Theatre of LA revival of the hit musical *Cabaret* to rave reviews.

But her talents don't end there. Singing is one of her great passions. She has performed for audiences from North America to Europe, Iceland to Malaysia in musical theatre, concert performances, USO tours, and even the occasional foray into the recording studio. In 1999, Judy joined the rest of her Walton family to record *A Walton Christmas -Together Again*. Judy followed this with a CD of her own, Reflections which features a collection of standards and Broadway songs.

In her spare time, Judy indulges in a variety of sports: skiing, tennis, competitive horse jumping. She has also trained in flying trapeze, wing walking, and roller derby; and has earned two skydiving world records. She has competed three times on *Battle of the Network Stars* which led to appearances on *Celebrity Challenge of the Sexes* and two editions of *Circus of the Stars.*

And if all of that is not enough, she loves to cook for her husband and son. No question about it, Judy Norton is a force with which to be reckoned!

"My favorite childhood recipe was a dish my mom made. It always seemed like eating dessert for dinner because it was in a pie crust. She always made her pie crust from scratch, and it was delicious. Unfortunately, she never shared the secret to her amazing crust, but I love this dish.

I never thought of my mom as a great cook. Raised in England during the war, the meals that influenced her early years were simple, bland, and always overcooked! Of course, she always claimed it was us kids who weren't willing to try anything new…probably true. So the memory of this recipe stands out as extra special.

Judy's Mom's Corned Beef Hash Pie

Preheat oven to 400 F
2 15oz cans Corned Beef Hash, Cook until lightly browned
1 double 9" pie crust
Place cooked corned beef hash in the bottom crust
Optional:
1 10oz. bag of fresh spinach, washed and stemmed
Cook spinach just until it wilts
1 Tbsp butter
Melt in a small frying pan
1 small onion, chopped
Saute in butter until onion is soft. 1 clove garlic, minced
Drain, stir into spinach and layer mixture on top of corned beef hash.

Staying with the "pie" theme, I decided to share my quiche recipe. I love to modify recipes, so this one is a version of a recipe I came across at some point. Having what some might consider "picky" food tastes, I often change recipes to swap out ingredients I'm not fond of for ingredients I like better. I started using this quiche recipe when I was having guests over and wanted something ready to go. I recently served it Thanksgiving day. I had a couple of girlfriends coming over to help with the prep for the big turkey dinner. Knowing we would be slicing and dicing and all that goes into preparing all the fixings, I wanted to have something we could snack on for lunch without having to stop and fix yet another dish. So, the night before, while baking pumpkin pies, I also made this quiche. It was a big hit, and I've continued to prep it in advance of the need for a great, quick meal.

Judy's Calico Quiche

Preheat oven to 400 F

    1 10oz. bag of fresh spinach, washed and stemmed.
    Cook spinach just until it wilts.
    Drain well and chop coarsely.
    1 Tbsp butter melted in small frying pan.
    1 small onion, chopped, Sauté in butter until onion is nearly soft.
    8 oz. mushrooms sliced then add mushrooms to cook lightly.
    1 clove garlic, minced.
    Drain, stir into spinach and set aside.
    1 9" pie crust Place crust in a deep 9" pie plate.
    12 oz. cooked sausage (of your choice) Cut in bit size pieces. Layer in bottom crust.
    1 ½ cups grated Swiss cheese.
    Sprinkle ½ the cheese evenly over the sausage.
    Layer spinach mixture over cheese. Top with remaining cheese.
    ½ orange, ½ yellow pepper cut in short Julienne strips.
    Lay in circle over cheese.
    2 Tbsp. grated Parmesan cheese sprinkled on top.
    5-6 eggs beaten.
    ¾ tsp. dried tarragon leaf.
    Stir into beaten egg and pour into pie.
    Bake 25–35 min or until egg is cooked."

Jon Walmsley

Born in England, Jon emigrated to the U.S. with his parents and began his performing career at the age of 8, singing and playing guitar. Spotted by Hollywood producers on a local TV talent show, Jon was soon appearing in commercials and television shows such as *Combat, Daniel Boone, My Three Sons, Nanny and the Professor, The Bill Cosby Show, Adam-12*, and the Disney musical feature film, *The One And Only, Genuine, Original Family Band*. He also created the voice of Christopher Robin for the Academy Award-winning featurette, *Winnie-the-Pooh and the Blustery Day*. But Jon is best remembered for his warm and rich portrayal as Jason, the second oldest son in the Walton clan during his 9-year run on *The Waltons*.

Along with his acting career, Jon continued to develop his musical skills, writing and performing many original songs for *The Walton*s. At 19, he made his debut on the *Grand Ole Opry* and has since appeared as a guitaristand vocalist on television, records, and stages around the world with such diverse and legendary artists as Richard Marx, Brian Setzer, Dave Koz, The Doobie Brothers, Gregg Allman, Merle Haggard, Roy Acuff, John Mayall, Denny Laine, Spencer Davis, Peter & Gordon, Jackie Lomax, Roger Daltrey, Eric Johnson, and Strawberry Alarm Clock – just to name a few. Jon's solo debut blues album *Goin' To Clarksdale* was released in summer 2017 to enthusiastic reviews. Television session credits include *Home Improvement, Seventh Heaven, Roseanne, Boy Meets World, Beverly Hills 90210, The Waltons, Eight Simple Rules, Secret Life of the American Teenager.*

In 2018, Jon and his wife, Marion, returned to the UK (which he left at the age of 2) and now live in retirement on the coast of North Cornwall in the South West of England. The popularity of *The Waltons* never wanes, and he still makes appearances with his TV family to this day.

"I grew up in a very British household. It just happened to be located in Southern California. One of my mother's specialties was this most English of desserts—Sherry trifle, a delightful combination of fruit, spongy ladyfingers, pudding, cream, and, well, the sherry doesn't hurt either. Cheers!

Jon's Traditional English Trifle

1 5.1 ounce package instant vanilla pudding
3 cups whole milk cold
1-pint heavy cream
1/4 cup sugar
1 1/2 teaspoons vanilla extract
7 ounces ladyfingers crunchy (if using soft, see note below)
1/2 cup Sherry wine
1 12-ounce package frozen mixed berries thawed
2 quarts fresh strawberries hulled and sliced
1/3 cup sliced almonds toasted, cooled

Make pudding by mixing a 5.1-ounce package with 3 cups of cold milk (if your package has different measurements of milk, follow those).
Whisk to combine until it's thickened. Place in the fridge to thicken a little more until we need it.
Make whipped cream by adding heavy cream, sugar, and vanilla to the bowl of a mixer.
Beat with a whisk attachment until thickened and stiff peaks form.
Set aside.
Layer 1/2 of the ladyfingers on the bottom of a trifle dish.
Slowly pour 1/4 cup of Sherry wine over the ladyfingers.
With a slotted spoon, scoop half of the thawed mixed berries over the ladyfingers.
They should be strained enough with the spoon, but don't worry if a little extra juice gets in there.
Layer 1/2 of the prepared pudding over the berries, making sure that they are completely covered.
Add 1/2 of sliced strawberries over the top of the pudding.
 If you want a nice presentation, you can line the edge with strawberry slices standing straight up.
Layer 1/2 of the whipped cream over the strawberries, completely covering them.
Repeat layers.
Sprinkle toasted almonds (that have cooled) over the top layer of whipped cream.
If the almonds are still warm, they will melt the whipped cream, so make sure they have cooled.
Let the mixture set in the fridge for at least 2 hours before serving (ideally overnight, if possible).

*If using soft ladyfingers, toast them in a 350-degree oven until they're slightly browned on top, about 5 minutes. This will help them absorb the Sherry a little better without getting soggy.

*You can toast the almonds by placing in a 350-degree oven for 5-7 minutes until slightly browned. This lasagna is one that Marion and I like to make together. The secret weapon here is the homemade pasta. It tastes so fresh and just melts in your mouth. While we are pressing the dough, we usually put on some Dean Martin, drink Italian wine and do a little dancing in the kitchen. Molto romantico!

Walmsley Mushroom and Fresh Herb Lasagna

12 No-Boil lasagna noodles or fresh lasagna pasta sheets
1 Qt Milk
½ Cup unsalted butter
½ cup Flour
1 ½ teaspoons Kosher salt
½ teaspoon pepper
½ Nutmeg
3 Garlic cloves, minced
3 tablespoons chopped parsley, divided
1 tablespoon chopped fresh thyme, divided
2 medium Leeks, Sliced into thin rings
1 ½ lbs. portabella mushrooms, sliced
½ lbs. Shiitake mushrooms, stemmed and sliced
1 cup finely shredded parmesan cheese
1 cup plus 2 tablespoons coarsely shredded asiago cheese

Soften noodles in a pan of very hot water while you prep the other ingredients.
Alternatively, make fresh pasta dough.
Make béchamel (white sauce): Bring milk to a simmer in a saucepan and remove from heat.
Melt butter in a large saucepan over medium heat.
Add flour and cook, stirring until slightly darkened, 2 minutes.
Whisk milk into flour mixture all at once and whisk until smooth.
Add 1 ½ tsp salt, ½ tsp pepper, and the nutmeg.
The sauce should be thick enough to coat a spoon;
if it isn't, cook over medium-low heat, stirring, until thickened, 2 to 3 minutes.
Remove from heat and stir in garlic, 2 tbsp. parsley, and ½ tbsp. thyme.

Keep covered.
Preheat oven to 375F. Heat a deep, wide
pot over medium-high heat 2 minutes.
Swirl in 1 tbsp. oil and add leeks. Cook
until tender but not browned, 3 to 4
minutes, stirring occasionally.
Scoop leeks in a bowl and set aside.

Swirl 2 tbsp. oil into the pot.
Add mushrooms, season lightly with salt
and pepper, and cook over medium heat,
covered, until mushrooms are tender
and beginning to release juices, about 5
minutes.
Uncover and cook until edges start to
brown.
Stir in leeks and remaining ½ tbsp.
thyme. Remove from heat.
Mix parmesan with asiago.
Assemble lasagna:
Oil a 9- by 13-inch baking dish.
Spread a few spoonfuls of
béchamel over the bottom.
Arrange 3 noodles crosswise
in dish, then spoon on about ½ cup
Béchamel, follow with a third of the
mushroom and 1/3 cup of cheeses.
Repeat layers twice more.
Top with a final layer of noodles and
béchamel and sprinkle with remaining
cheese.
Bake lasagna until browned and bubbling
about 45 minutes.

Sprinkle with the remaining 1 tbsp. parsley and let sit at least 15 minutes before slicing.

If you have a pasta machine, I definitely recommend making fresh pasta sheets:
2 ½ Cups unbleached all-purpose flour, more as needed
4 large eggs, at room temperature
Kosher Salt

Mound flour on a clean work surface and make a well in the middle.
Crack eggs into the well.
With a fork, lightly beat the eggs, gradually pulling flour from the inner rim into the egg until a soft, clumpy dough begins to form.
When the dough becomes difficult to work with the fork, use your hands to pull in the remaining flour from the well, kneading gently until dough is cohesive.
Knead dough until it becomes smooth, elastic and just a bit tacky, about 5 minutes.
Cover with a towel and let rest at room temperature for 20 minutes.
Cut dough into 6 pieces and pass each piece through your pasta machine, starting at the widest setting and reducing it until the pasta is about 1/16 inch thick and 3 inches wide (usually around setting 7).
Bring 10 Qt. pot of well-salted water to a boil.
Put a large bowl of Ice water near the pot of boiling water.
Line a rimmed baking sheet with two clean kitchen towels and have more towels ready.
Put 3 or 4 noodles into the boiling water.
Cook for about 30 seconds.
With a large wire skimmer, carefully transfer them to the ice water to stop the cooking.
Repeat with the remaining noodles.
Drain noodles and spread them flat on the towel-lined baking sheet.
Layer the noodles between clean towels and set aside until you're ready to assemble the lasagna."

What's Happening!!

What's Happening!!, loosely based on the film *Cooley High*, follows the lives of three African-American teens living in Watts. The show stars Ernest Thomas as Roger "Raj" Thomas, an aspiring writer, and Fred Berry as Freddie "Rerun" Stubbs. Danielle Spencer co-stars as Raj's younger sister Dee with Mabel King as their mother Mabel; and Shirley Hemphill as Shirley Wilson, a waitress at Rob's Place, the neighborhood hangout.

It originally premiered as a summer series in August of 1976; and returned as a weekly series from November 1976 through April 1979 on ABC for a total of 65 episodes. From 1985 to 1988, a sequel series titled *What's Happening Now!!* aired in first-run syndication with most of the major cast members.

On the left: Raj, Rerun and Dwayne

Ernest Thomas

In person, Ernest Thomas is hilarious, his big smile and infectious laugh lighting up any room he occupies. He is best known for his acclaimed roles as Raj from *What's Happening!!* and *What's Happening Now!!* and Mr. Omar in *Everybody Hates Chris*. Born in Gary, Indiana, he earned a Bachelor's Degree of Science in Sociology and Psychology from Indiana State. With few opportunities in Gary, he moved to New York to pursue acting. He began his professional career on Broadway in 1974 in a play produced by the legendary Hal Prince and starring Glenn Close. Not a bad start. The following year, he again worked with Ms. Close on the Great White Way. After graduation from the prestigious American Academy of Dramatic Arts, Ernest decided to seek his fortune in Los Angeles in 1975.

He found work quickly, guesting on shows like *Baretta*, *The Brady Bunch*, and *The Jeffersons*. It was during the taping of *The Jeffersons* that Isabel Sanford's agent told Ernest about an audition for a show called *What's Happening!!* Ernest was chosen over more than 200 actors. Opportunities for work abounded after its three-year run. The first was a role in the hit urban comedy *Piece of the Action*. Sidney Poitier chose him to star in it alongside Bill Cosby and James Earl Jones. Equally adept at drama, Ernest just missed being cast as Kunta Kinte in the award-winning mini-series *Roots*. Instead, he played Kailubu, a role written expressly for him.

In 1985, Ernest was invited to reprise his role as Raj in *What's Happening Now!!* After its successful three-year run, he made appearances in *The Parent 'Hood, Martin, Soul Food,* among others. In '92, he starred with Oscar winner Denzel Washington in Spike Lee's biopic, *Malcolm X*, a film recently placed in the U.S. National Film Registry by the Library of Congress because of its cultural and historical significance.

After touring in theater, Ernest returned to sitcom stardom as Mr. Omar, the funeral director, in *Everybody Hates Chris*, the award-winning series created by comedian Chris Rock.

In 2007, he starred in *Paroled* with Spider Loc, Candy Ann Brown, and Master P. He was featured in Adam Sandler's *Funny People* (2009); and in Rob Zombie's 2012 film, *The Lords of Salem*, among others.

Ernest received the Best Actor Award from Beat TV in 1979 and a nomination in 1987 for an NAACP Image Award for his role as Raj. In 1992, he won the MPAC (Muslim Public Affairs Council) Award for his role in *Malcolm X*. He has received numerous honors from congressmen, mayors and clergymen for his outstanding work with various charities. Muhammad Ali chose him as a featured speaker for the Muhammad Ali World Hunger Tour. His ability to bring diverse groups together was never as apparent as when he organized the first joint press conference against apartheid between Muslim Imams and Catholic priests in Washington, D.C. He was also a keynote speaker at the event. With more than 30 years of achievement in theatre, television and film, *TV GUIDE* chose him as one of America's favorites in the issue titled "Stars We Still Love" in 1996. In his off-screen time, Ernest writes screenplays, manages new talent, and mans a production company, Bravokid Entertainment. He wrote a book with his mother entitled *Conversations with My Mother: Food for the Mind, Body and Soul.* In 2017, his autobiography was released. From *Raj To Riches: Overcoming Life Through Faith* is a motivational story about how to overcome show business and life through faith….and through laughter, definitely through laughter…"Laughter and comedy by any means necessary."

"Campbell's Tomato Soup was my favorite soup as a kid in the Doris Miller Projects in Gary, Indiana. My mother and grandmother were amused by my obsession with tomato soup. My other favorite was a hot dog on a slice of white Wonder Bread with mustard. The idea came to me one day: a slice of the hot dog in the tomato soup — and it was love at first taste.

Ernest's Tomato Soup with Hot Dogs

Cut hot dog into small pieces, place in a pot of soup. Heat together and eat with crackers.

About 20 years ago, salmon became a favorite. It was served to me at a small take-out restaurant in Ontario, California. The owners were from Turkey, I believe. It was well-seasoned and grilled and I fell in love with it. I asked my friends who cooked how to do it. I also looked at recipes in cookbooks and then just seasoned it according to my taste.

Grilled Salmon a la Ernest

Season the salmon with garlic powder and Lawry's seasoning salt. Grill. Heat a little lemon juice with butter and spread it on top. I always have steamed broccoli, cauliflower and carrots with it with lemon juice and garlic, parsley and pinch of salt. I could eat that every day, and plus, it's healthy for you."

Epilogue

Mad Men's Don Draper defined nostalgia as "a twinge in your heart far more powerful than memory alone." That says it. We carry these marvelous TV Classic kids in our hearts along with the drive-ins and ice cream parlors in which they ate. You needn't have lived in Los Angeles to relate to the restaurants they mentioned. Places like that were in every town all across the USA.

Sometimes I have to pinch myself. As a child growing up in St. Louis watching all my favorite TV friends, I never dreamed I would be fortunate enough to call them my "real-life" friends as an adult—much less marry Timmy from *Lassie*!

Life is full of surprises, and, as I came to know these child stars personally, one of the biggest surprises was what their off-camera lives were really like. As a child, I never thought about what they did on-camera as actual work. I had no idea of the adult responsibilities they carried on their small shoulders. It's been quite an education and has only made me appreciate them that much more. For some, it was a difficult journey; but back then, there was nowhere for them to turn for direction or advice. These were the first generation of television child stars. There was no blueprint to follow. Most of their parents were flying by the seats of their pants. Paul Petersen of *The Donna Reed Show* recognized their needs and filled the void with his exceptional organization, *A Minor Consideration*, which has helped countless young performers navigate the rough waters of show business and beyond when the phone stops ringing. He has so generously given back to his community. I am happy to give a portion of the profits from *TV DINNERS* to AMC.

www.aminorconsideration.org is a non-profit foundation created to provide guidance and support for young performers, past, present, and future. With an emphasis on education as well as advocacy for legislation designed to ensure that young performers actually receive the monies they earn, AMC is on-call to assist parents and their professional children on a no-cost basis. Additionally, members of AMC are always available to help with the tricky transition issues that prove to be so troubling for many child performers. We've "been there, done that." Our lessons were earned, not imagined.

Acknowledgements

I want to thank the child stars of classic television who so generously contributed to this book. Because of them, these pages abound with warmth and humor; and our childhood memories are filled with joy.

Photo Credits:

Page 9: Jeanne Russell; p. 11-12a: Jon Provost; 12b: author; p. 14: Jeanne Russell; p. 16-17: author; p. 19: ABC; 20-4 Paul Petersen; p. 25: author; p. 26: CBS; 27: Billy Gray; p. 28: author; p. 31: ABC; p. 32: Jerry Mathers; p. 34: DuPar's; p. 35: Jerry Mathers; p. 37: Tony Dow; p. 39: author; p. 41: Lucie Arnaz; p. 42-5: Keith Thibodeaux; p. 46-7: Wrather Corp; p. 48-9: Joey Vieira; p. 52: Annette Funicello Collection; p. 54: AIP; p. 55-7: Annette Funicello Collection; p. 59-62: Sharon Baird; p. 64, 66: Disney Studios; p. 67: David Stollery; p. 68-70: author; p. 71-3: Beverly Washburn; p. 74: C.C. Brown family; p. 77-80: Veronica Cartwright; p. 82-3: Larry Mazzeo; p. 84: author; p. 87, 89: Kathy Garver; p. 91-2, 94: Philip Goldberg; p. 95: author; p. 97: 20th Century Fox Television; p. 99: Marc Copage; p. 101-4: Jon Provost; p. 105: Ronephoto; p. 108: Bill Mumy; p. 109-112: Angela Cartwright; p. 115-8: Bill Mumy; p. 120-3: Cynthia Pepper; p. 125, 127: Qualis Productions; p. 126, 128-9: Schultz Bros; p. 131: CBS; p. 132-4: Butch Patrick; p. 136: Don Fedderson Prods; p. 137-141: Stanley Livingston; p. 142-4: Barry Livingston; p. 145-6: Dawn Lyn; p. 148-9: ABC; p. 150: Martin Grams; p.153-4: Michael McGreevey; p. 155: Disney Studios; 156: Michael McGreevey; p. 158: DuPar's; p. 161: Cayuga Prods; 162-5: Morgan Brittany; p. 170: ABC; p. 172: Barry Williams; p. 174: Spelling-Goldberg; p. 175-7: Kris McNichol; p. 179-80: Parker Stevenson; p. 183-5: Radames Pera; p. 187-9, 191: Wesley Eure; p. 192-4: Kathy Coleman; p. 195-6, 201: Alison Arngrim; p. 202: ABC; p.204-5: Pamelyn Ferdin; p. 206-9: Judy Norton; p. 211-2, 215: Jon Walmsley; p. 217: ABC; p. 218, 220: Ernest Thomas

What are some of your favorite foods, places, shows, recipes and memories?
Please share them on our Facebook Page:
https://www.facebook.com/TVDinnersBook/